CAIN'S LEGACY

Also by
Jeanne Safer

CAIN'S LEGACY

Liberating Siblings from a Lifetime of
Rage, Shame, Secrecy, and Regret

Jeanne Safer, Ph.D.

BASIC BOOKS
NEW YORK
A Member of the Perseus Books Group

Published by Basic Books,
A Member of the Perseus Books Group

Books published by Basic Books are available at special discounts for bulk purchases in the United States by corporations, institutions, and other organizations. For more information, please contact the Special Markets Department at the Perseus Books Group, 2300 Chestnut Street, Suite 200, Philadelphia, PA 19103, or call (800) 810-4145, ext. 5000, or e-mail special.markets@perseusbooks.com.

Typeset in 12 point Adobe Caslon Pro by the Perseus Books Group

Library of Congress Cataloging-in-Publication Data

Safer, Jeanne.
    Cain's legacy : liberating siblings from a lifetime of rage, shame, secrecy, and regret /
Jeanne Safer.
        p. cm.
    Includes bibliographical references and index.
    ISBN 978-0-465-01940-3 (hardcover) — ISBN 978-0-465-02944-0 (e-book)
    1. Brothers and sisters. 2. Families. I. Title.
    BF723.S43.S127   2012
    306.875—dc23
                                                                            2011028959

10 9 8 7 6 5 4 3 2 1

For Harriet Wald,
my sister by choice

Fraternal love, sometimes almost every thing, is at others worse than nothing.

—JANE AUSTEN, *Mansfield Park*

Hostile feelings towards brothers and sisters must be far more frequent than the unseeing eye of the adult can perceive.

—SIGMUND FREUD, *The Interpretation of Dreams*

When we step into the family, by the act of being born, we do step into a world which is incalculable, into a world which has its own strange laws . . . into a world that we have not made.

—G. K. CHESTERTON, *Heretics*

CONTENTS

Author's Note

The names and identifying information of everyone interviewed in this book have been changed.

ACKNOWLEDGMENTS

I want to thank the siblings I interviewed for sharing their experience with me with such depth and candor. Talking to them about this taboo topic was revelatory for me. I am indebted to my agent, Michelle Tessler, for her unfailing encouragement and clearheaded advice and to my editor, Thomas Kelleher, for his appreciation and expertise. Lara Heimert, editorial director of Basic Books, eased my way. My research assistant, Jessica Brinkforth, was tireless. Dr. Douglas Mock generously, wittily, and patiently gave me an informal tutorial in evolutionary biology and corrected many a misconception in my chapter on his specialty. Thanks to Joan Arnold, Dr. Cindy Baum-Baicker, Trudy Crandall, Dr. Paul Ehrlich, Dr. Barbara Kapatanakes, Amanda Moon, Rabbi Leonard Schoolman, and Dr. Nina Smiley for enthusiastic backup during the entire project and to my husband, Richard Brookhiser, for seeing me through it, as he always does.

My deep gratitude goes to Dr. Anne Hallward, host and creator of Safe Space Radio and a woman after my heart. She believed passionately in my project and personally recruited some of the most articulate, insightful subjects any author could wish for.

This book is dedicated to Harriet Wald, my dear friend and colleague, whose generosity, warmth, and unconditional love have sustained me for over three decades. She is the sister I wish I would have had.

INTRODUCTION
The Secret World of Sibling Strife

✢

I had an older brother, but he was never a brother to me. We spent our childhoods at the same address with the same biological parents, ate dinner at the same table every night, and even shared a room for a few years at first, although we never shared a single confidence while we occupied it. We had the same coloring, the same body type, some of the same talents. But the universes we inhabited never intersected, and our parents were the same people in name only. Our relationship, begun in simmering mutual resentment, progressed to rare obligatory meetings, and ended in complete estranged silence. Although I made some futile attempts, I could never be a sister to him, and I did not grieve when he died at age sixty-four. Only a year later, when I happened to attend a concert of the vintage jazz he loved and performed, did I find myself weeping uncontrollably for what we never had.

⁜

At least one-third of the adult siblings in America suffer serious sibling strife like mine—the number rises significantly, to 45 percent, when clinicians probe more deeply. Instead of feelings of kinship and warmth for their nearest relatives, these brothers and sisters feel secret shame, rage, guilt, resentment, alienation, contempt, or, worst of all, more cold indifference than a stranger could ever evoke. Frozen in time, frozen in place, they cannot be their adult selves in their adversary's company. Nobody thinks or talks about this predicament because nobody knows what to do about it. We convince ourselves that problem siblings—many of whom seem perfectly normal except when they are driving us crazy—don't matter once we leave home and no longer live under the same roof with them, that they have no further impact on our lives. Denial tends to wear off over time, however; the majority of adult siblings, when questioned late in life, confess that they feel worse about unresolved relationships with brothers and sisters than about any other unfinished business. Eighty-five percent of Americans have siblings, and because these ties last longer than any others—fifty to eighty years is the norm, compared to the thirty to fifty years most people know their parents—and 90 percent of people over sixty-five still have at least one living sibling, that's a lot of regret. I wrote *Cain's Legacy* to explore that regret, to relieve it, and, when possible, to transform it.

The trials of life with a mentally or physically dysfunctional sibling was the topic of my partially autobiographical book

The Normal One, but as the powerful and revealing stories told by the sixty beleaguered adults of all ages I interviewed for *Cain's Legacy* demonstrate, the phenomenon is far more widespread than that. A brother or sister need not be incapacitated to cause trouble.

Why are sibling woes so disturbing and so recalcitrant? Our first peer relationship has the deepest roots of all, and you can't get a divorce. Problems between husbands and wives derive from childhood experiences, but problems with siblings *are* childhood experiences in contemporary guise. Rivalry, competition, and anxiety about your place in your parents' affections underlie these problems, breeding rancor that haunts siblings all their lives and recurs in each phase of adulthood—work, marriage, parenthood, caring for aging parents, and, eventually, settling that perpetual minefield, the estate. The mutually injured parties (at least those who still maintain a precarious connection) walk on eggshells, loathe to confront each other for fear of precipitating an unfixable breech. As a result, their discord goes underground, only to reemerge in times of crisis, with mutually assured destruction.

Sibling strife is nothing like the normal fighting between brothers and sisters who basically get along. These opponents never make up; there is not enough goodwill to counterbalance their perennial grudges. Always on the defensive and in management mode, strife-ridden siblings never feel natural in each other's company; they cannot be playful together or comfort each other. They even talk to each other in a special language, which I have dubbed "Sibspeak," in which words are weapons rather than modes of communication. They view family occasions with foreboding and joint decision-making with dread. If you also have simpatico siblings the contrast is excruciating, but if your only sibling is estranged you cannot imagine what brotherly or sisterly tenderness feels like. You may try—often successfully—to find surrogates with whom to imitate that instinctive intimacy, but it is never quite the same. Far beneath the surface, as I discovered, there still lurks a secret hunger for the fundamental security that loving family ties provide, a sanctuary forever inaccessible when your sibling cannot be your friend.

The hopeless pain that sibling strife provokes is the only remaining taboo topic in contemporary life: the black box—as well as the Pandora's box—of family problems. We don't even let ourselves dream about it very much. Thinking about problem siblings always goes to the bottom of the to-do list, somewhere after cleaning the closets, because most people—and until quite recently, most psychotherapists—believe the fallacy that dealing with difficult brothers and sisters is optional. But you can never escape them because they are part of you.

Whether you make peace, never speak to each other again, maintain a chilly civility, or vacillate between love and hate, you're stuck with this relationship—at least inside yourself—for the rest of your life. You can and do have a choice whether to interact but not whether to be influenced by them; it is a fait accompli.

Even if you haven't seen them in decades, troublesome siblings accompany you everywhere—the bedroom, the professional meeting, the cocktail party. They are psychically present when you work with a colleague, when your friend has a triumph or a failure. Collaboration, competition, making friends and losing them, bear their marks. So do your own children, who evoke them all over again. They subtly influence your most important relationship choices—including whom you marry—almost as much as parents do. They provide the template for much of adult life and its discontents.

Not only are they our constant internal companions, but the worse the relationship, the more potent and hidden it is. Nonetheless, one hundred years after Freud discovered the central importance of childhood experience in defining character, siblings remain terra incognita. Otherwise thoughtful, self-reflective adults have "no idea" why they're not close to a brother or sister. They use external explanations to rationalize their aversion ("We live in different cities," "He's a Republican," and "I can't stand her husband" are typical excuses), without realizing that none of these things would keep them and their siblings apart if they wanted to be together.

Unless you understand your adversary as a person with a view of the world and of you that is radically different from your own, you cannot fully understand yourself. We cut off a part of ourselves when we ignore these siblings; they come back to haunt us when we thrust them away. Even if we cannot love them and find interacting with them toxic or infuriating, we owe it to ourselves to think about them in a new way. *Cain's Legacy* shows you how.

I wrote this book to bring these troubling, long-neglected life companions into the spotlight where they belong, because only then can we begin to make sense of our relationship with them. By looking at them rather than looking away we can figure out what went awry and perhaps have a chance to change course, or realize why we never can, but sealing the relationship off leaves it forever unresolvable. This field guide to problem siblings shows you how to understand who they are, why they act the way they do, and why you react the way you do, which permits you to see the relationship from a new perspective. And should you decide to try to connect or re-connect, you will find out how to go about it—including what not to do or say.

Siblings who fail to confront their childhood hurts—for all serious strife has childhood roots—inevitably drift apart or become permanently estranged, stuck in a disturbing rela-tionship they can neither comprehend nor alter, its meanings forever locked deep within the estranged partners. Even those who long for reconciliation have no idea how to proceed, or are too frightened and angry to try.

The insights offered here cannot create love, but can help neutralize hatred and alter the inner landscape that siblings inhabit. Whether the final destination is rapprochement, man-agement, or well-considered rejection, and even if only one partner participates, this book provides a road map to navi-gate unexplored terrain and the guidance of a sibling "couples counselor" who is both a sister deeply familiar with strife and a psychotherapist who specializes in the unique struggles siblings face.

In addition to plants, animals, and the matriarchs and patriarchs of the Book of Genesis—the natural world and the world of the Bible are hotbeds of sibling strife—here are some of the siblings you will meet:

- A dermatologist who agonized over her need to ask her far-less-successful sister for a kidney transplant
- A journalist who struggled to decide whether to liquidate her savings to prevent her ne'er-do-well brother from foreclosing on his mortgage
- A teacher whose mother left her entire estate—including the family home he helped build—to his sister, who had no qualms about accepting it
- Two sisters who are currently laboring to overcome the sadomasochistic relationship they had as children and to appreciate each other as adults

Most therapists and authors of books on siblings have a bias—sometimes unconscious, sometimes clearly stated—toward reconciliation, and they make it sound far easier than it often proves to be. Ignoring siblings has now been replaced with a compulsive need to embrace them, no matter how they act or how we feel. Most authorities encourage unquestioning acceptance of the conventional wisdom that family ties are always worth preserving because "blood is thicker than water"—a mantra that reflects the pernicious trend in contemporary society toward universal, unconditional forgiveness. On the contrary, I have found that sometimes this substance is too toxic to absorb; not all betrayals, even by our closest relatives, can be forgiven, nor should all siblings be welcomed back into one's world. This book will help you figure out how to know the difference.

Cain's Legacy reflects my passionate conviction that it is essential not to gloss over the dark side of life. We must acknowledge how difficult these relationships really are in order to address effectively the obstacles they present. Facing reality is a great relief for siblings who feel like failures when they cannot resurrect their relationships even if they follow all the instructions and exhortations they find in the existing literature.

I do believe—because I have seen it and assisted siblings in achieving it—that reconciliation can happen even when the bonds are severely strained and anger goes deep, but both parties have to want it badly enough to do the hard work it entails. Some people I interviewed have transformed or are attempting to transform decades-long deadlocks into living, and even loving, connections. Others have made the rational and self-enhancing decision never to see their offending relatives again. Both kinds, and many gradations between these extremes, tell their stories here. Not "being close" to your closest relative is always a loss, but it is often a necessary or unavoidable one. This book will help you to determine your own truth.

Regardless of how siblings behave or what role we grant them in our adult lives, gaining perspective is always possible. Whatever the outcome, confronting the causes of sibling strife is arduous but rewarding; it is guaranteed to reveal secrets you keep from yourself. The process will transform your relationship to your history and will help you recognize the real human being who shared it, often for the first time. Then, even if you cannot become friends, you can cease to be enemies.

⊹

When you look in the mirror, your difficult sibling always looks back, though the image is distorted. In the shadows lurk parts of yourself and your past that you don't want to notice. Behind the reflection, silently influencing the interaction, stand your parents, your grandparents, and all their siblings. If you learn to look you can understand them all.

I hope this book opens your eyes.

CHAPTER I

BACTERIA, BOOBIES, AND THE BIBLE

A Brief History of Sibling Strife

⁜

I. Wild Siblings

Sibling strife has been a fact of life for a long, long time. It's much older than sex. Siblings (defined by evolutionary biologists as any genetically related peers, from the unicellular up to and including us) were at one another's throats before they had throats. It started with bacteria and continues throughout the phylogenetic scale. From microbes to humankind—even plants are not exempt, but they move slowly enough that their brutal and occasionally lethal competition is harder to detect— sibling strife is the norm. Of course, there are also bonds of affection—wolf cubs take good care of each other (at least as long as food is plentiful)—but that's the nicer side of nature.

Siblings naturally vie with each other from birth for food and parental attention and protection, sometimes to the death; parents collude or look on as their offspring attack or kill each other in their battle to prevail. Humans, although their conduct is typically more restrained, have not improved significantly on this behavioral design.

"Siblicide," a term popularized by evolutionary biologist Douglas Mock to describe the most extreme form of sibling rivalry, and also known as "Cainism" after the first biblical brother-slayer, is a fact of life for many species. The deadly efficiency of the infant perpetrators and the insouciance of their mothers and fathers is hard for humans—even scientifically trained ones—to accept. Although our own species is hardly immune, murder and cannibalism clash with our family values, as well as with the assumption formerly widespread among biologists that protecting all their offspring is always a parental priority.

Mock disproved this comforting notion serendipitously. When rough waves prevented him from observing the great egrets he was studying in the wild on an island where the colony bred, he had to hand-raise them in artificial nests. Then he noticed the hatchlings "jabbing each other" with their sharp beaks. The youngest of four sons himself, he assumed both from his childhood experience and from prevailing theory that watchful egret parents would naturally behave like his human ones had and step in to curb the mayhem ("Parents won't allow this, I confidently announced," he recalled), so he created mock-parents out of pillowcases stuffed with dried leaves to police the orphan chicks. However, when the waves calmed, his assistant was able to observe actual nests from a blind. Mock described the far more chilling scenario he learned of via walkie-talkie. "'What's going on out there?' I asked in excitement. 'Broods are fighting like hell!' my assistant Rick replied. 'What are the parents doing?' was my very next question. 'Nothing, they're just standing there watching!' he responded."

Not only did the real egret parents lift nary a wing, but they actually yawned in boredom as their firstborn chick viciously pecked the youngest one and often succeeded in evicting it from the nest, where the parents ignored its piteous begging. What he saw changed his mind. "I realized that the whole drama is from a script written and directed by the parents," he concluded. "The young are brutal, systematic, and relentless in their attacks on siblings. The parents are relatively ineffective (or uninterested) in their efforts to minimize the impact of that rivalry." What looked like inaction was actually tolerance or collusion with brood reduction. Mock has an incriminating yawning-egret photograph to document the adults' depraved indifference. "That photo embodies the most unexpected thing I've discovered during forty years of fieldwork," he told me.

Since relative ease of observation makes birds a favorite subject for field study, research has now repeatedly confirmed that the blasé egrets are far from the only neglectful and complicit avian parents. Many species do not intervene when an older sibling pecks a younger one to death or inflicts wounds that hasten its demise.

The family values of the blue-footed booby, whose star-tlingly hued webbed feet and quizzical expression delight visitors to the Galapagos, are notorious; booby parents stand idly by as the first booby baby pecks and ejects all others sib-lings from the nest to die of predation or starvation. The ma-jestic golden eagle is no more kindly disposed; eaglet number one dispatches eaglet number two by casting it out from their lofty nest, in full view of the adult birds. Its nearest relative is this fuzzy little predator's first victim. These raptors mean business; a firstborn African black eaglet was observed to ad-minister a total of 1,569 blows from its hooked beak during thirty-eight assaults on the secondborn one, which died in three days. Contrary to their heart-warming reputation—the film *The March of the Penguins* got kudos from political conservatives—not all penguins are model parents; in one of the most extreme examples of favoritism from the very be-ginning, Magellanic penguins hatch two chicks, but feed only one. And why are those kookaburras laughing? Because as youngsters they used their temporarily hooked bills—the weapon nature provides expressly for the job—to intimidate their nestmates in order to procure for themselves the best tidbits their parents have to offer. The chicks are so intent on fighting that they don't stop when researchers pick them up to take measurements.

Charles Darwin noticed, among other disturbing observa-tions, that most animal siblings are not intrinsically kind to one another, and this has now been documented in all manner of creatures. "Whenever two or more offspring depend on resources provided by parents, sibling rivalry kicks in automatically," says Mock; "human family dynamics are a special case of a ubiquitous phenomenon."

For newborns of every species, the first order of business is looking out for number one by securing maximum parental resources for oneself; in the competition for survival, the goal is insuring that you're the fittest. The urge to be the favorite child—or the only one left—by any means necessary rules. What soon-to-be-civilized human babies fortunately commit mostly in fantasy, many of our pseudopod-ed, winged, and four-legged forebears act out literally, with no guilt at all. Evolution determines the "script" that animal parents follow; memory as well as innate behavior programs people.

In animals that practice siblicide, firstborns have a head start. The advantage of size and strength helps the elder destroy younger potential competitors and become the parents' heir apparent; with its parents' implicit permission, the elder sibling does the dirty work. In the obligate type of siblicide, practiced by boobies, pelicans, and others, killing younger rivals is automatic; in the more frequent facultative variety, foul play occurs only when food is scarce. Humans notoriously reverse the natural order of things, as the book of Genesis recounts; the youngest child, often at the behest of the mother and with her assistance, frequently becomes the favorite.

Like the kookaburra, even many of the lowliest life forms are equipped with ingenious weapons specifically designed to maim or kill their nearest and dearest. Colonies of the bacteria *Paenibacillus dendritiformis* engage in internecine chemical warfare. Related aggregates cohabiting on a nutrient substance mutually inhibit the growth of their sibling-foes by secreting a lethal antibacterial compound. Bacteria facing each other at the edges of both colonies are destroyed; as in humans, neither side emerges unscathed.

Despite their loathsome reputation, leeches are among the simplest organisms that care for their young. Australian brood-tending leech parents (*Helobdella papillornata*) provide meals of microscopic gastropods—and the differences in size and heft among their miniscule offspring indicate that the plumper ones snatch more snails than their slimmer kin.

Family behavior gets no cozier as it gets more complex. Forest trees compete for lebensraum and sun slowly and relentlessly, but the Bad Seed Prize must go to the Indian rosewood (*Dalbergia sissoo*), a tree whose wood is among the world's loveliest. When its pods are still attached to the mother tree, the first seed to sprout (the one farthest from the tree) exudes a poison that moves toward the stem, silently killing every one of its podmates within weeks.

Sharks are the hands-down winners in the monstrous sibling sweepstakes: Even before they're born, they practice not only murder but also cannibalism. Biologist Stewart Springer made this creepy discovery when he was dissecting a ten-foot-long female sand tiger shark and had his finger nipped by a toothy embryo that was still swimming in utero. The first egg to hatch in each of the predator's two uteruses dispatches and dines on all its wombmates with its fully functional teeth so that only the two biggest babies survive.

We expect sharks to behave like sharks, but we harbor utopian fantasies about the domestic arrangements of other creatures. The beehive epitomizes ideals of communal living, altruism, and cooperation. But even in this utopia, rivalry between sisters can turn lethal; in their attempts to usurp the throne, wannabe queens sting their sisters to death. There is nothing PC about the natural world.

Spotted hyenas, on the other hand, are true to their image, biting same-sex twins with such brutality that 25 percent of them die of their wounds. Cute little pink piglets, who we think should be better behaved because they are domesticated, are equipped at birth with vicious baby teeth. They use them to defend their favorite teat from infant porcine usurpers by slashing their faces; farmers routinely clip these weapons to prevent injury to the sows' udders. In both cases, the mothers—who were sibling winners themselves—never object. Family life is unfair, from womb to tomb, and its inequities are continually reproduced.

⚓

If the behavior of our unicellular, vegetable, avian, and mammalian predecessors has anything to teach us, it is that intense, often murderous sibling rivalry is built into life on earth and that human beings, whatever else they are, are no exception. Selfishness precedes the capacity for empathy. Of course, our forebears are not prey to the ambivalence, guilt or the longing for connection that plagues human siblings and complicates their relationships; they are driven only by the imperative to survive. But we, like they, are aggressive at the core, as are our parents, most of whom are also siblings. This research makes clear that intense competition for limited resources (in our case, emotional as well as physical nurturance) is not only part of nature but also a fundamental part of human nature.

Relations between brothers and sisters are at their violent worst when the young are competing in close quarters—as in a nest, a den, or a human nursery. This hostility within the family assures efficient resource allocation—that the parents will have no more offspring left than they can effectively provide for. It is not going to disappear anytime soon. Therefore, despite many human parents' tireless efforts, siblings without rivalry are an impossibility. Siblinghood is deeply fraught, even when we don't fight to the death. Adult humans are as complicit as the yawning egrets. They pick favorites and offer love selectively, causing rivalry to fester long after their own demise.

Human sibling relationships have a built-in dark side; pretending it's not true only drives it underground. Turning a blind eye, as the boobies do, won't stop it; management, rather than elimination or denial, is the only realistic goal for both parents and children. Loving siblings is an achievement, brought about in large part by how their parents handle the inevitable conflicts among their children. The success of their efforts is determined by how the parents—and their own parents—handled the conflicts intrinsic to their own family life. Since sibling strife is here to stay, our best psychological tools to deal with it are conscious recognition, acceptance, and understanding.

II. Biblical Siblings

In the beginning, there was sibling strife. It is the one phenomenon that evolutionary biology and the Bible agree on. Parents, from bystanding boobies to the Patriarchs and Matriarchs, either passively comply or actively incite it. But, as the book of Genesis graphically depicts, only the human ones push their chosen heirs with cunning and passion, reversing the pattern of biologically programmed "primogeniture" that is the norm in the rest of nature. Unfair parental behavior—including God the Father's—and the sibling strife it engenders are principal themes in Genesis, reverberating through the generations, contaminating relationships between brothers, sisters, whole, half-, and step-siblings alike.

Biblical siblinghood is steeped in conflict. One is either murdering the other (Cain versus Abel), stealing his legacy (Jacob versus Esau), or her mate (Leah versus Rachel), or their parent's love (Joseph versus his brothers). Empathy is rare, and reconciliation among strife-ridden siblings, when it does come, is poignant, late, and hard-won.

Genesis depicts many varieties of family dysfunction, where the role of both God and mortal parents is ambivalent, usually more selfish than wise. But the text also offers a few moving portrayals of conflict resolution, even when grievous or criminal wrongs have been committed. In those remarkable instances when nearly catastrophic conflicts are actually worked through, it is via independent action by siblings who in maturity eventually achieve insight and experience remorse.

CAIN AND ABEL

Soon after the first sin, disobedience, gets Adam and Eve expelled from Eden, the first crime, siblicide, is committed by their eldest son. The murder seems virtually provoked by God, who accepts the baby lamb offered by their younger son, Abel, but rejects the first fruits that Cain brings Him. God takes the original parental role in the first family. For no reason that commentators have been able adequately to explain for millennia, "The Lord regarded Abel and his offering but He did not regard Cain"; He favors the shepherd over the farmer.

God sets a terrible—and much-imitated—example for all human parents. Why couldn't He, as a benevolent father, notice, accept, and appreciate Cain as well as Abel? Their temperaments and talents may have been different, but both of the first two siblings gave what they had, both needed and deserved recognition for their hard work and their sincere devotion. Even if He was more drawn to one, couldn't He have made the effort? Instead, God does what many fathers have done since: He abdicates His own responsibility for turning Cain against Abel and adds insult to injury by blaming the victim/ aggressor, failing to acknowledge that Cain has any reason to be angry in the first place, and warning the son He rejected about the potential for sinning that His own unfair treatment has enflamed rather than assuaged. Instead of helping Cain manage his justified anger and avert disaster, He shows no empathy and offers nothing but threats and blame. God says:

> *Why are you incensed,*
> *and why is your face fallen?*
> *For whether you offer well,*
> *or whether you do not,*
> *At the tent flap sin crouches*

The first parent figure's favoritism is as flagrant and destructive, and his motives as inexplicable, as any human parent's.

After Cain murders Abel and God confronts the perpetrator, He behaves with surprising leniency. Why doesn't He strike Cain dead for his crime? Later in the narrative, God destroys the entire cities of Sodom and Gomorrah to punish the depravity of their inhabitants and also kills Onan for "wasting his seed"*—surely a lesser offense than murdering one's innocent brother in cold blood. Although He does banish Cain and condemn him to be a "restless wanderer," God not only spares Cain's life but also gives him a mark of protection to

---

* According to Robert Alter, this phrase refers to coitus interruptus rather than masturbation, as it is commonly translated.

prevent anyone else from harming him. Eventually, the curse seems to be revoked because Cain is permitted to marry, have a son, and found a city in the land of Nod, becoming a patriarch in his own right, whose descendants become the founders of music and toolmaking. Could this tolerance be evidence of God implicitly acknowledging His own role in provoking Cain to commit the murder?

The mark of Cain is typically misunderstood as a stigma, a disgraceful indication of criminality rather than a protective charm against vengeance, but in fact it is both. It symbolizes the hatred and self-hatred, the envy and sense of alienation, as well as the shame and guilt that keep many rejected children from feeling they have as much right to recognition as other people—especially their own favored siblings—do. Those who carry it are both criminals and victims. Foregoing your identity as the child who was overlooked involves acknowledging your wish—even if you take no overt action—to harm your more successful competitor. Loving and working despite the mark that sets you apart break the curse.

Unfairly favored children who seek to recover their siblings must also acknowledge that their own actions perpetuate Cain's mark, though only their siblings bear it overtly. They are compelled to justify having been chosen over their siblings and have a stake in remaining so. Mutual recognition can ultimately neutralize parents' original arbitrary choices and allow real brotherhood or sisterhood to flourish. Very few siblings achieve this either in the Bible or in the outside world, but those who do so prosper.

ISHMAEL AND ISAAC

The troubled family life of Abraham, the first Patriarch, depicts the perils of step-parenthood, a common occurrence in Genesis. It is a case study of the roles parents play in perpetuating sibling strife, of maternal jealousy and paternal passivity, here complicated by God's own mixed messages and ambivalent actions. Abraham's wife, Sarah, is barren, so she arranges for him to have sex with a surrogate, her slave Hagar. But when Hagar conceives and acts superior to her mistress— or Sarah thinks she does—Sarah complains to Abraham ("This outrage against me is because of you!"), who, in order to keep the peace, lets her harass and expel her pregnant rival. God, rather than softening Sarah's heart or strengthening Abraham's resolve, sends a messenger to tell Hagar to return and "suffer abuse" for the sake of her unborn son, Ishmael's, future greatness. Later, after Sarah's own son, Isaac, is born, she observes Ishmael mocking him. Taking an insult to her child as a personal affront, as mothers often do, and wanting to secure Isaac's inheritance and her own position by getting rid of the competition for good, she demands that Abraham banish Hagar and Ishmael. When Abraham has second thoughts ("The thing seemed evil in Abraham's eyes"), God intervenes and persuades Abraham to override his scruples and permit this act of cruelty for his own future gains, saying, "Whatever Sarah says to you, listen to her voice, for through Isaac shall your seed be acclaimed." To compensate Ishmael for being rejected by his father and losing his family and his home, God promises to make Ishmael head of a nation of bellicose outsiders, "his hand against all, the hand of all against him." The fallout from this arrangement still rages with undiminished ferocity among these siblings' descendants in the modern Middle East.

ESAU AND JACOB

In the next generation, the story of the brothers Esau and Jacob, the Bible's first set of twins, illustrates the consequences when both parents play favorites; Isaac identifies with one brother and his wife, Rebekah, with the other. Although God prophesies before they are born that Esau, the elder, is destined to be his younger brother, Jacob's, slave, it is their mother's active conniving and their father's obliviousness that almost provoke a second siblicide. Each parent picks a son to meet narcissistic needs and through whom to act out competitive issues with each other—Isaac favoring the hirsute herdsman Esau and Rebekah preferring Jacob, the more refined homebody. One brother is impulsive, the other wily.

Jacob, an entitled mother's darling, robs his brother twice, with no compunction or remorse. First he makes the famished man trade his birthright for lentil stew. Later he allows Rebekah to disguise him as Esau in order to trick their blind father into bestowing upon him the blessing traditionally meant for the firstborn. To assure that he will feel and smell like his brother, Rebekah covers Jacob's smooth arms with goatskin and dresses him in Esau's clothes. She also prepares a faux-venison stew (she has Jacob bring her a kid from the flock) for Jacob to serve to his father, who had requested a game dish from Esau. A mother with a mission, she stops at nothing to push her favorite, never considering the effect of her actions on the brothers' future relationship.

Isaac is taken in by this deception because he really does not know either of his sons intimately. He only differentiates them by their external characteristics, like the fake Esau's hairy arms and the smell of his garments. Hearing Jacob's voice issuing from "Esau's" mouth only momentarily confuses him. Since his blindness is psychological as well as physical, he quickly accepts the "game" stew and blesses the wrong son. Only what a son can provide for him matters to him.

When the real Esau returns from the hunt with Isaac's favorite dish and the deception is revealed ("Who are you?" Isaac asks him), Isaac does not recant. "Blessed he stays!" he says, further confirming his limitations as a father. Once Isaac changes allegiances, he has nothing more to give. Isaac completes the entire family's betrayal of Esau, offering him neither material nor emotional compensation; he simply accepts his son's plight as fate and shows no real regret.

The desperate Esau begs for some legacy, some morsel of love. "Do you have but one blessing, my father? Bless me too, Father," he says, twice reiterating their relationship. What Isaac gives his former favorite instead is more like a curse:

> *By your sword shall you live*
> *and your brother shall you serve,*
> *And when you rebel*
> *you shall break off his yoke from your neck*

Even a son who, despite his loyalty and physical prowess, is reckless and uncouth, deserves better than this.

But, remarkably, the prophecy is not fulfilled; this saga does not lead to brotherly bloodshed. Rebekah spirits Jacob away to her brother's estate until things calm down—he ends up marrying and raising a family there—but time and distance alone would not suffice to neutralize such hatred. Esau, through his own emotional development, becomes the first wronged sibling in the Bible to get over it. Simply and directly, he shows his brother that he has forgiven him.

The reconciliation between Esau and Jacob is remarkable. Twenty years after stealing Esau's blessing, Jacob flees from his father-in-law and has to travel through his brother's territory. Justifiably worried that Esau, now a powerful chieftain in his own right, will try to kill him and his retinue in revenge, Jacob sends messengers with flocks as tribute. But when he hears that Esau himself is coming with four hundred men to meet him, Jacob assumes that he is going to be attacked and begs God to "save me from the hand of my brother." Trembling with terror, he bows to the ground seven times before his twin, as if approaching royalty. His family and retainers also bow.

But there is no need for divine protection or obeisance because Esau, true to his impulsive nature, lovingly extends the very arms that Jacob pretended were his: "And Esau ran to meet him and embraced him and fell upon his neck and kissed him, and they wept." He addresses Jacob affectionately as "my brother," while Jacob, true to his cautious nature, behaves with anxious deference throughout their encounter, referring to himself as "your servant" and using only formal, ultrapolite language when addressing Esau. He offers Esau the tribute himself, "to find favor in the eyes of my lord."

The brothers then have a dialogue that few estranged siblings ever achieve. At first Esau refuses Jacob's extravagant gesture, saying, "I have enough,* my brother. Keep what you have." Despite having been deprived of his birthright and his blessing, Esau is satisfied with what he has achieved in his own right. When people have what they need emotionally, they do not envy what others have—even brothers who have cheated them out of what by rights was theirs. Flawed but ultimately wise, Esau is the rare sibling who has not spent his time resenting the unfairness of his childhood and plotting revenge—which really would have made him his brother's slave—but has gone about living well instead as the head of his own clan.

Jacob then makes heartfelt recompense. This time he presses Esau to accept his gift not to placate him or offer material goods for a spiritual loss but to serve as an act of acknowledgment and contrition: "O, no, pray, if I have found favor in your eyes, take this tribute from my hand, for have I not seen your face as one might see God's face, and you received me in kindness? Pray take my blessing that has been brought you, for God has favored me and I have everything." He admits that he has an unfair advantage and finally in gratitude

---

* The Robert Alter translation of *The Five Books of Moses*, which I have been quoting, translates Esau's words as "I have much, my brother." This is one place where I believe the King James version is more psychologically accurate, if less literal.

and even, perhaps, humility gives Esau back the blessing he deserves but no longer needs.

At the end of their meeting, Jacob sensibly decides that he and Esau must part, even though Esau says, "Let's journey onward and go, and let me go along beside you"; they can reconcile, but intimacy is impossible. They have nothing in common, and having wronged Esau so grievously, Jacob can never quite relax in his company. Jacob finds a tactful pretense for them to go their separate ways by claiming that his children force him to travel at a slower pace and promises to meet Esau at his headquarters in Seir, which he has no intention of doing; Jacob actually heads in the opposite direction to Succoth and builds a house there. Still not quite trusting that his brother has truly forgiven him—or that he deserves to be completely forgiven—Jacob also refuses Esau's offer of men to accompany him. The two brothers have healed the past but cannot be soulmates or have a future together. The next time they meet is to bury their father, as is true of many siblings with problematic relationships.*

---

* After their reconciliation, both brothers live for a time in Canaan, until Esau moves "to another land away from Jacob." Although the text gives population density as the cause for their final separation ("For their substance was too great for their dwelling together, and the land . . . could not support them), this, like Jacob's stated reason for declining to travel with Esau initially, is only an external explanation. The previous narrative implies that psychological incompatibility is the real reason they must end up living far apart. Esau's descendants are enumerated after he moves, and he never appears again.

LEAH AND RACHEL

Leah and Rachel, the Bible's most famous battling sisters, do not fare as well as their mutual husband, Jacob, and his brother, Esau; their sibling strife never ends. Their relentless envy-fueled competition, though it is manifested differently because they are women, poisons both their lives, embitters their marriages, and makes their children hate each other. It even contributes to Rachel's premature death.

After he cheated Esau and fled to his uncle Laban's homeland, Jacob met and immediately fell in love with his cousin Rachel. Since he had no dowry to offer, he traded Laban seven years of labor for her hand. He awoke from the bridal bed to discover her older sister Leah, whose "tender eyes" were her only good feature, beside him instead.

Although the text says that Laban "took his daughter Leah and brought her to Jacob," Leah herself, who was not a slave but his legitimate child, must have given her consent to the substitution (Laban had previously asked her aunt, his sister Rebekah, whether she wanted to become Isaac's bride). One-upwomanship was already going strong between the unlovely Leah and her alluring younger sister, and this was her chance to steal Rachel's betrothed the only way she could. But the plan backfired painfully. After only one week of marriage, she lost out to her sister. Jacob, furious and resentful, agreed to work for Laban for another seven years to get the woman he really wanted and was allowed to marry Rachel. Although Leah eventually bore him six sons, Jacob always preferred his first choice and "despised" the usurper.

There is nothing subtle about the sisters' sex and mother-hood war. Leah spends her life trying to get blood from a stone, competing with Rachel for the husband they have to share. As many women have done before and since, she consoles herself by boasting that she is extremely fertile, while her sister is bar-ren. Each time she gives birth, she hopes the new son will fi-nally endear her to Jacob; she declares, "Now my husband will love me," then "This time at last my husband will join me," and later "This time my husband will exalt me." She even bases the names for her sons on the Hebrew words for these phrases, a daily living reminder of her feelings. But it never works.

Meanwhile, Rachel, despite her beauty and her success in love, is insanely jealous of her sister's prodigious fecundity; each sister believes the other has something essential that she lacks herself. Desperate to narrow Leah's 6–0 lead, Rachel commands Jacob, "Give me sons or I'm a dead woman," mak-ing him "incensed" with her and predicting her own premature demise. She and her sister use their cohusband as a sperm donor in their ongoing maternity contest, which has a per-sonal, vindictive edge well beyond the universal desire for male heirs that was normal in their culture.

The sisters even enlist their slaves as surrogates to continue the fight. When her slave conceives twice, Rachel triumphantly and shamelessly announces (and commemorates the news in her proxy son's name), "In awesome grapplings I grappled with my sister and yes, I have won out." But Leah, not to be un-done despite having four sons already, offers her own slave, who delivers two sons, evening the surrogacy score.

When one of Leah's sons provides her with mandrakes, a fertility aid, so that she can continue reproducing, Rachel begs her for some. At first Leah refuses, saying bitterly as well as untruthfully, "Is it not enough that you have taken my husband, and now you would take the mandrakes of my son?" She accuses Rachel of stealing her husband, when in fact it was the other way around. Rival siblings distort the facts to fit their feelings and deny their own provocative actions; only their grievances register. She then makes a humiliating deal with Rachel, "hiring" her own husband for the night in return for the mandrakes, and of course she conceives again.

When Rachel finally does give birth to the son she longs for, she exclaims, "God has taken away my shame," suggesting that avoiding further humiliation by Leah is as important to her as motherhood. Rachel is so caught up in the competition that she names her son Joseph, which means "May the Lord add me another son." She can't even enjoy the child she has but immediately wants another—and the second childbirth, which produces Benjamin, kills her. Neither of these sisters ever feels she has enough.

Leah is so intent on stealing her sister's husband that she cannot think of the discord she will have to endure for the rest of her life as a result because they all live in close quarters. She refuses to face reality and clings to the hopeless, pernicious fantasy that she can mean more to Jacob than her sister does, which she never has and never will. All her efforts cannot make Jacob love her, but do guarantee that her sister will hate her.

Leah's obsession with Rachel and her own sense of inferiority make her reproductive victory pyrrhic and causes endless acrimony among their family members, the ones who
always suffer collateral damage in a sibling feud. Her venge-
ful act prevents her from ever finding a man for whom she
could truly come first or be valued in her own right. The price
she pays is never to appreciate what she has; even her many
sons become mere weapons in the overriding task of best-
ing her sister. Unlike Esau, who went his own way and found
fulfillment despite his brother's becoming the chosen one,
this elder sibling remains her younger sister's victim; bearing her own version of Cain's mark, she lets Rachel define
her life.

Neither Rachel nor Leah can ever know each other as human beings, or find any common ground. Each is blinded by
her obsession with what she considers the other's assets and
her own deficits. As long as she lives, Leah is reminded of her
inferior status in her husband's eyes; fearing Esau's attack
after fleeing from Laban, Jacob arrays the slaves and their
sons in the most exposed position in front, then Leah and her
sons, but he protects Joseph and Rachel by putting them at
the back out of harm's way. Sibling strife causes Leah to forfeit her pride and Rachel to eventually forfeit her life.

The sisters' compulsion to outdo each other rules them;
nothing else matters or even registers. This futile ambition
prevents either one from having an intimate relationship with
her own husband or children, let alone with each other; everything and everybody else is a means to the end, which, be-

cause it is based on overcoming a feeling of defectiveness within each of them, can never be satisfied. They bequeath a legacy of envy and enmity to their children.

Biblical commentators have long noted that Jacob's penance for his unfair victory over his brother is to be forced to spend most of his adult life tormented by the unresolved rivalry between his wives. But Leah and Rachel are each other's penance.

JOSEPH AND HIS BROTHERS

Rachel's son Joseph and Jacob's ten other sons by Leah and the sisters' slaves (Joseph's full brother, Benjamin, is still too young to be involved) inherit and continue their mothers'—as well as their father's—sibling strife. The account of how both sides laboriously transform a relationship destined for catastrophe and become true brothers is unparalleled in its dramatic power and profundity. More than any other siblings in Genesis, they make mutual reparation based on mutual recognition. After their arduous reconciliation, Joseph even tries to prevent their father, Jacob, from perpetuating the divisive tradition of parental favoritism with his grandsons, Joseph's two sons. Joseph fails, but he achieves the insight that is a prerequisite for change in future generations.

This ancient depiction of the travails of a blended family has striking contemporary relevance. The jealousy a first wife's children feel when their father dotes on the much younger child of his second marriage is magnified enormously here because the second wife is the first wife's more desirable younger sister, the one their father wanted all along.

Joseph—gifted, arrogant, and "comely to look at"—is the Bible's premier dream interpreter and psychologist. We first meet him as a narcissistic seventeen-year-old flaunting his father's blatant preference for the "child of his old age" who is also a reminder of Rachel, Jacob's dead beloved. Extreme parental preferences can often be explained but are irrational nonetheless, just as Rebekah's predilection for Jacob over Esau had been. As chosen children are wont to do when they become parents, Jacob identifies with the young son who feels as entitled as he himself once did, which blinds the father to the impact of his behavior both on his other children and on his favorite. Replicating his own experience seems so natural that he never questions or even notices the outcome; even when Jacob is on his deathbed, Joseph will come first with him.

Rather than attempting to conceal his partiality, Jacob advertises it. He goes so far as to make and present to Joseph the beautiful "coat of many colors," a literal mark of favor that ends up marking his boy for murder by his envious half-brothers. This extravagant, thoughtless gesture exacerbates the seething resentment his other sons already feel—and it also encourages Joseph, with his sense of superiority, to behave in ways guaranteed to provoke them. The text says bluntly and repeatedly, "The brothers saw Jacob loved him more, and they hated him."

As a teenager, Joseph was his father's agent, bringing "ill report" of his brothers to Jacob—a role he would reproduce later in life when powerful men came to rely on his exceptional abilities. But as a youth, he was obnoxious, precocious, and oblivious, a self-important tattletale. He told his outraged brothers first one offensive dream in which their sheaves of wheat bow down to his and then another in which the entire universe, including the sun, the moon, and eleven stars (which he and his audience recognize as representing the brothers and their parents), bows down to him. Not surprisingly, his brothers feared that "he means to rule over us." He also shamelessly told his father this second dream, which took Jacob aback; it reflected grandiosity and presumption so like his own, however prophetic the content turned out to be.

Even though Jacob should know better, he sends Joseph off in his ostentatious outfit to "see how your brothers fare," and this time the information-gathering errand turns out to be fateful. The brothers decide to kill the "dream-master," stripping off his hateful tunic and throwing him into a pit. Two of them, Reuben and Judah, have scruples about murdering him outright; Reuben suggests leaving him for dead but intends to retrieve him later, and Judah recommends selling him into slavery as punishment for his presumption, which the brothers decide to do. Leaving Joseph trapped, they go off to have a meal. In their absence, merchants pull him out and sell him themselves. Joseph ends up in Egypt, where he is purchased by Pharaoh's chamberlain, Potiphar. This trauma and the hardships as well as the extraordinary triumphs of his life there over the next two decades turn him into a man of "wisdom and discernment."

When Reuben returns to free Joseph, he finds the pit empty and assumes his brother is dead. The remorseless brothers bloody Joseph's tunic and send it home, leaving Jacob to conclude that his son has been killed by a wild beast. Jacob mourns Joseph extravagantly and longer than necessary, yet another indication of his preference.

Joseph's Egyptian master soon recognizes the unusual abilities of his slave and turns over the running of the household to him, which he does with great competence until Potiphar's wife falsely accuses the compelling young man of rape and has him thrown into prison. There he distinguishes himself once more, and the warden puts him in charge of the other prisoners. When Pharaoh has two terrifying nightmares that none of the official soothsayers can explain, a former fellow inmate whose dream Joseph had correctly deciphered recommends his services. His interpretation—that the dreams predict famine—so impresses Pharaoh that he makes Joseph his viceroy, and Joseph's assiduous planning prevents the population from starving while enriching the state treasury. This favorite son's ability to appeal to father figures never fails him. By the age of thirty, he has gone from slavery and imprisonment to a position of authority second only to Pharaoh.

Joseph's combination of brilliance, beauty, and executive flair help him prevail in every situation, and he becomes Egypt's savior, showered by the grateful sovereign with wealth, power, and an aristocratic wife, by whom he has two sons. To commemorate his suffering at his brothers' hands and his victory over it, he names his firstborn Menasseh ("God has released me from all the debt of my hardship, and all my father's house") and the younger Ephraim ("God has made me fruitful in the land of my affliction").

But the story does not end there. His siblings come back to haunt him, as siblings always do.

When the famine of Pharaoh's nightmares comes to pass, it spreads throughout the region, including Canaan, where Joseph's family lives. Jacob sends all the brothers but Benjamin—he cannot bear the possibility of losing Rachel's only other son—to buy food in Egypt, even though they are loath to go. There, just as Joseph's dream predicted, they prostrate themselves before the viceroy, whom of course they do not recognize, although he recognizes them and "remembers his dream."

Joseph then orchestrates a series of trials and corrective emotional experiences that symbolically reenact in reverse what happened to him. Through them the brothers experience the full brunt of their crime and the guilt, grief, and remorse that were lacking when they committed it, and they are given the opportunity to redeem themselves. Both they and he change dramatically as a result.

Like an initiation rite performed under his guidance, the ordeals, with their repeated reversals of fortune and their dialectic of safety and danger, innocence and guilt, are intended to induce a state of anxiety and heightened awareness in the perpetrators. Though he is in complete control of their fate, Joseph is deeply engaged in the scenario of sublimated vengeance that he produces and directs; emotion frequently overtakes him as he witnesses his brothers' evolving changes of heart. The result is the birth of empathy in both them and him.

⚜

As his brothers unwittingly make obeisance to him upon arrival—they use the same obsequious language that Jacob used with Esau, but accurately and without Jacob's calculation, calling him "my lord" and referring to themselves as "your servants"—Joseph plays the harsh and suspicious stranger, speaking through an interpreter and accusing them of spying (as he once did on them) and throwing them in prison (where he once languished himself) for three days. At first, he announces that he will test "whether the truth is with you" by detaining all of them except the one he orders to fetch their youngest brother, Benjamin, whom he secretly longs to see.

Joseph quickly relents, however, keeping only Simeon hostage and allowing the others to go home with food. Will they faithfully return and risk death for their brother's sake? Joseph has to turn away and weep when he overhears his guilt-ridden brothers lament that they are paying for their depraved conduct toward him in the past; their genuine remorse forms the foundation for future forgiveness. On their way home to Canaan, the brothers discover to their horror that the silver they used to pay for supplies has been put back in their bags—Joseph's way to frighten and assist them simultaneously—and they fear that they will be accused of stealing if they ever go back to Egypt.

Their constant comings and goings, obeisances, pseudo-thefts, and threatened enslavements are like a recurring dream from which they cannot extricate themselves. Joseph keeps creating situations for them to feel what was missing in the past.

The famine continues. When the provisions are exhausted, Jacob tells his sons to travel back to Egypt to buy more, but they refuse to make the trip unless Benjamin accompanies them, as Joseph commanded. Clinging to the old favoritism, Jacob says, "My son shall not go down, for his brother is dead and he alone remains"—as though none of the others is also his son. Reuben, still reckless, proposes that his own two sons be killed if he fails to bring Benjamin back safely. But Judah, with new maturity and conscience, offers to be his young brother's "pledge" and swears to Jacob to "bear the guilt to you for all time" if Benjamin is harmed—demonstrating concern for his father's feelings and his brother's welfare that were absent the first time around—and Jacob relents.

When they arrive back in Egypt, Joseph has all eleven brought to his house for a meal, a highly unusual invitation. To avoid being imprisoned for theft, they confess to his servant that the silver they paid has mysteriously reappeared in their baggage. He tells them to keep it because "your God" put it there and further reassures them by setting Simeon free. They bow to Joseph once more, but when he sees the brother he thought he had lost forever, he rushes from the room to weep in private.

The viceroy keeps his brothers continuously off balance. At the feast, he seats them by birth order and gives Benjamin five times as much food as the others, displaying knowledge meant to seem uncanny. Though they all get drunk together, he still does not reveal his identity and has his silver goblet hidden in Benjamin's belongings as a pretext to arrest them all yet again.

The next morning, Joseph's servant overtakes the brothers as they start for home, declaring, "You have wrought evil in what you did," and accuses them of stealing Joseph's divination vessel. Acknowledging their guilt for the far more terrible crime that they actually did commit years before, they swear that the culprit shall die and the others shall become Joseph's slaves; they submit to the fate to which they once condemned him.

To test their loyalty and fraternal sense of responsibility, the servant claims that only the thief will be enslaved. But when the goblet is discovered in Benjamin's bag, they are grief-stricken at the prospect of his servitude, as they never were over Joseph's fate. This time, instead of coldly abandoning their helpless brother, they return to Joseph's house and throw themselves at his feet once more. Their spokesman, Judah, takes responsibility for the "theft" and confesses their old sin— "How shall we prove ourselves guiltless? God has found out your servants' crime"—offering that they all should become his slaves.

Joseph, pursuing his own agenda, refuses to enact so harsh a penalty ("Far be it from me to do this") and frees everyone but Benjamin. Judah, a changed man, then steps forward and pleads that Jacob will die without his youngest son. The man who was indifferent to his father's feelings when he recommended selling one brother into slavery now offers to become a slave himself as a proxy for the other.

Judah's self-sacrifice and compassion move the viceroy so deeply that he can remain incognito no longer. This time, he clears the room and weeps openly before them as their equal, saying simply, "I am Joseph, your brother, who you sold into Egypt." The sound of his passionate sobbing—tears of catharsis, grieving, and incipient love—carries all the way to Pharaoh's palace.

At first his brothers are dumbstruck. Grandiose no more, he comforts, forgives, and absolves them. "Do not be pained and do not be incensed with yourselves that you sold me down here," he says, explaining that God sent him ahead to "ensure your survival on earth and to preserve life, by a great deliverance." He also says that they "must tell *my* father of all my glory in Egypt"; the singular pronoun shows that he still sets himself apart from them. Even if he is no longer unbearably arrogant, he has not become humble; old habits need not die completely. After he and Benjamin embrace and cry together, he kisses all the brothers and "weeps over them." A father as much as a brother to his elders, he promises to "sustain" them in Goshen "close to me"—because this is a true reconciliation, there is no need to keep them at a distance as Jacob kept Esau.

But the Bible is a mirror of human nature, not a fairy tale. As he sends the brothers back to Canaan loaded down with provisions and commanded to bring Jacob to him—and once again giving Benjamin five times as much as the others—Joseph cannot help admonishing them to "see that you don't have a falling out along the way"; he recognizes their weaknesses and still feels compelled to point them out. Just because siblings reunite doesn't mean they have personality transplants.

Nor are suspicions about formerly estranged siblings ever entirely allayed. After Jacob dies in Canaan and his sons bury him with full honors, the brothers return to their new Egyptian home under Joseph's protection. Once there, they worry all over again that he will seek revenge, saying to one another, "If Joseph still bears resentment against us, he will surely pay us back for all the evil we caused him"; since vestiges of their old guilt linger, they assume his reaction will be unchanged as well. They send him a message—perhaps fabricated for the occasion—that before his death Jacob commanded them to formally ask for forgiveness ("We beseech you, forgive, pray, the crime and the offense of your brothers, for evil they have caused you"). This speech causes Joseph to weep yet again. Once more they bow to him ("Here we are, your slaves"). The past is never completely forgotten, envy and distrust can still be reignited, and the discrepancy between their stations in life is an unchangeable fact.

Joseph rises to the occasion. "Fear not," he tells them. "Am I instead of God? While you meant evil towards me, God meant it for good"; Joseph, at long last, is no longer a narcissist. Despite the enormous power he now wields in reality, not just in dreams, he knows its limits. His youthful hubris has mellowed; the ordeals he put his brothers through have chastened him as well. He recognizes that his unbridled arrogance and provocative behavior, which his father's partiality encouraged, made his brothers hate him; he, too, bears some responsibility for the past. He "reassures them and speaks to their hearts" and afterward keeps his word to sustain them and their families for the rest of his life. When Joseph finally dies at the age of 110, he asks them to swear that his remains will be moved to the promised land, and they, too, keep their word. Genesis, which begins with fratricide, ends with imperfect but fulfilled brotherhood.

⁂

Even though none of us are viceroys of Egypt with the might and the resources to design elaborate scenarios to make our straying siblings see the light, the narrative of Joseph and his brothers reveals essential emotional truths about the sibling healing process. It provides insights and guidelines to follow—including all the bumps along the way—for sisters and brothers attempting to redeem their relationships:

- Parents are always implicated in serious sibling strife. The circumstances that lead to violence in Joseph's family—the hatred and desire for vengeance that his brothers feel toward him and his contempt for them— were created and abetted by their father Jacob, based on his experiences in his own family before they were born.
- The text says that Joseph "recognizes" his brothers first; he sees more than they do, symbolically as well as literally. This is not just because he is Pharaoh's right- hand man and an adopted Egyptian speaking a language

they cannot understand. He has more insight, so he initiates the process, as the more psychologically minded sibling often does.

- On the surface, the power differential between Joseph and his brothers is enormous, and he is indisputably the one in control. But—as the tears that regularly overtake him reveal—he is as caught up in the relationship as his brothers are. Once siblings are engaged in the reconciliation process, the course is unpredictable for everyone concerned, and nobody has the upper hand or knows in advance where it will lead. There is always a large element of improvisation, miscalculation, and surprise when people attempt to repair damaged relationships.
- Although it is rare indeed for anybody to be blameless in sibling strife, one side is frequently more responsible for the rift than the other or behaves worse; there are plenty of obnoxious, grandiose adolescents, but their older brothers don't usually conspire to kill them. Joseph also comes to see his own contribution to this poisonous situation and to realize how outrageously he provoked and threatened his brothers—an essential step to reconciliation.
- Resolving sibling strife always involves mourning for losses, one of the meanings of Joseph's many episodes of weeping.
- Sometimes, as in the case of these brothers, caring for or mourning for a parent can bring siblings together.

- Only in the movies does lifelong animosity melt away in one tearful embrace. The most enduring lesson of the Joseph story is that resolution is a process that takes time, repeated efforts, and often repeated failure before anything shifts. Considering where these brothers started—and the burden of their family's history—it is miraculous that they were able to accomplish as much as they did.

EPHRAIM AND MANASSEH

Embedded in the saga of Jacob's sons is an incident about his grandsons that has come to have such great significance for sibling relations that it is evoked weekly in Jewish ritual. After the twelve brothers are initially reunited and settled in Egypt, Joseph learns that his father is ill, and he goes to visit him with his sons, Manasseh and Ephraim. Now blind, as his own father, Isaac, was when he was tricked into blessing the wrong brother, Jacob announces that he wants to bless his grandsons and adopt them to replace his sons Reuben and Simeon, presumably because their lawless behavior has made them unworthy to be heads of the family as Jacob's firstborn and secondborn heirs. The adoption will also make Joseph, his perennial favorite, progenitor of two tribes of Israel, while all the other sons get just one.

Joseph brings Ephraim, his younger son, to Jacob's left side and Manasseh, his elder, to his father's right, the traditional place for the firstborn to stand to be blessed, but Jacob crosses his hands so that his right hand rests on the younger son's head and his left (which bestows the less potent blessing) on the elder's. When Joseph sees that his father's hand positions indicate that he plans to give the younger son the blessing meant for the elder—as Isaac mistakenly did to Jacob and that Jacob symbolically bestowed on Joseph himself—"it was wrong in his eyes." Joseph now knows the consequences of over-the-top sibling preference all too well, and he says, "Not so, my father," as he attempts to uncross Jacob's hands and put them on the correct heads. But Jacob, intent on recapitulating the past, keeps his hands firmly crossed and says that Manasseh "shall be great, but his younger brother shall be greater than he," and reversing even their names, "set Ephraim before Manasseh" forevermore.

Jacob's act is typically interpreted as divinely inspired prescience—the reversal of primogeniture is a recurring theme in Genesis. But in psychological terms, it is a potent example of how the favored perpetuate favoritism in subsequent generations—often, as he does, justifying their choice with seemingly objective rationales—by identifying with one child and diminishing the other. Jacob persists in this behavior all his life; when he blesses his sons for the final time on his deathbed, he still singles Joseph out, reserving his longest and most all-encompassing blessing for the son he always considered "the one set apart from his brothers."

This episode may seem like a sidebar in the midst of Joseph's story, but in fact it exemplifies the underlying reason why healing sibling strife is so complicated: Parental preference sets up self-perpetuating conflicts that are unconsciously, and sometimes even consciously, played out and handed down, sowing dissent for future generations. Parents repeat with their children and grandchildren what happened to them. Joseph is the first one in his family to become conscious of the costs of compulsive, egregious favoritism. He objects and tries to prevent his father's doing to his grandchildren what almost destroyed Joseph himself, even though he is powerless to stop it. But he points the way.

To this day, "May God set you as Ephraim and Manasseh" is the blessing that Jewish parents pronounce over their children as Sabbath begins. It is said that the sons of Joseph are offered as a model for children because they are the first siblings in the Bible who are not locked in destructive sibling rivalry. If the goal were not so elusive, siblings through the ages would not have to be reminded every week to emulate them.

CHAPTER 2

ANIMOSITY BEGINS AT HOME

The Roots of Sibling Strife

⚔

Sigmund Freud committed siblicide. Since the founder of psychoanalysis was a civilized man, unlike Cain or the boobies, his weapon was a pen instead of a beak or a rock. The effects are still reverberating a hundred years later.

Freud's sin was one of omission, not commission; siblings were his blind spot in his work and in his life. The eldest of eight, his relationships with his own brothers and sisters were tragic and tumultuous. His first brother died at the age of eight months when Freud was a year and a half old, and six more rivals were born in quick succession—none of whom he mentioned in the autobiographical sketch he wrote late in life. Although he confessed in a letter to his best friend that his guilty, triumphant reaction to his brother's death "determined what is neurotic, but also what is intense, in all my friendships," Freud's twenty-three-volume collected works contain but five brief references to siblings. He erased them all, as though he were an only child. As a result, bitter rivalry—manifested in his need to be the center of attention, jealousy of potential usurpers, and vigilance about betrayal—bedeviled his relationships with colleagues and disciples for his entire career.

Paradoxically, it is not their insignificance that caused the first psychoanalyst to ignore his siblings, but rather his inability to deal with the emotions they evoked—feelings too radioactive even for the fearless explorer of the unconscious to investigate too closely. Generations of therapists have followed suit, with the result that parent/child relationships have been examined in depth for a century, while sibling studies have barely scratched the surface. Shakespeare, Dostoyevsky, Austen, and the authors of Genesis have done a much better job than psychoanalysts in illuminating sibling relations. By now everybody has heard of the Oedipus complex (the hostile competition between father and son for the mother's love), but Cain and Abel have yet to get a complex of their own. In fact, Freud may have focused his attention on father/son rivalry—omitting siblings from the proceedings entirely—to avoid the more dangerous threat posed by aggression and rivalry among children for their parents' affection, which he himself experienced daily. Even though my profession is beginning to figure out that brothers and sisters matter, we still have no road map for resolving what ails them. What cannot be named cannot be known.

What went wrong in the Freud family is the same scenario that produces strife-ridden siblings in many families, including the Safer family: extreme favoritism and mishandled ri-

valry coupled with subtle abandonment by frustrated, conflicted parents unconsciously living through their preferred
children. This treatment produces a potent brew of ambition,
confidence, self-absorption, and anxiety in the child who is
picked to be the bearer of a parent's destiny, and simultaneously breeds bitter resentment in the losers of the parental-
love competition—all of which goes underground. It casts a
pall over the siblings' relationships for life.*

A reminiscence written on the occasion of his death by
Freud's sister Anna,** who was two and a half years younger, reveals more than she realizes about the effect of their mother's
preference for her brother, and she gives a first-person account
of the blatant form that preference took. Family legends
prophesying Sigmund's fame, she notes, were often recounted
by their mother, who called him *"Mein Goldener Sigi* [my
golden little Siggy]."† Anna enumerates the unmistakable and
unfair privileges lavished on him alone—the private bedroom
(the six surviving siblings had to double up), the oil lamp to aid
his studies (the others had to make do with candles). His needs
overrode hers; when her brother complained that the noise

---

* Extreme favoritism is not the only scenario that produces sibling strife,
but it is of particular importance since it occurred so dramatically in Freud's
own family and its implications are so rarely explored. Other parental
pathologies (depression, hostility, coldness) certainly contribute to antagonism, but these problems can also cause siblings to bond; favoritism almost always severs them.

** Anna Bernays, "My Brother, Sigmund Freud," *American Mercury*,
November 1940, 334–340.

† She continued to call him Sigi into his seventies; there is no record of
a nickname for Anna.

Anna made when she practiced her piano bothered him—even though their rooms were on opposite ends of the house—the piano disappeared, and none of the other children were permitted to study music thereafter. In retribution some seventy years after the fact, Anna mentions gratuitously that Sigi could never carry a tune. She announces in another covert dig that she and her family had the foresight to emigrate to the United States long before the Nazis came to power, while he had to flee Vienna at the end of his life after the Nazis took over. Slighted siblings have long memories.

Only an unhappy parent favors one child over the others as outrageously as the Freuds' mother did. She clearly made her firstborn son the repository of her hopes for a variety of reasons beyond his considerable actual talents; he relieved her depression after the death of his infant brother and compensated her for her disappointment with her husband's business failures. His victory, as annihilating as it must have seemed to his child rivals, had to feel unsecure to him. As often happens in large families where money is scarce, her constant pregnancies preoccupied her ("If I'm so special," her eldest must have thought, "why does she keep having other babies?") and prevented her from paying adequate attention to the needs of all her children—which included being valued in their own right and having caring relationships with one another. Singling out a Golden One (and banishing his sister's piano) virtually guarantees sibling strife.

In another time and place, my own mother enacted a remarkably similar scenario, but it was I, her daughter and younger child, whom she selected for shockingly special treatment in order to replace her son and her husband, both of whom had failed her. Which child is chosen for this dubious honor depends on the parent's fantasies—some require a son or firstborn to be "their" child, while for others a daughter or the baby of the family fits that job description. My mother, who also identified with her daughter because she had been her own mother's favorite, bestowed a unisex pen name on the newborn repository of her hopes, whom she decided was destined to be a writer. The second bedroom that the siblings briefly shared—there were only two in the apartment—soon became her daughter's alone; her son was relegated to a room in the attic. She groomed her daughter to be her companion, her compensation, and her creation and was incapable of understanding the unbreachable chasm that her behavior created between her children. Her son never got over being rejected. Like Freud, her daughter grew up with a combination of self-possession and insecurity, unaware (at least on a conscious level) that her preferred status might be undeserved—a reflection of her parent's needs rather than her own merit. To this day, she fears the envy and enmity of her peers. There are always advantages to being the favorite child,* but they are never unalloyed, and no family in which extreme favoritism is practiced is a healthy one.

---

* Children who remember being even slightly favored report better well-being (including better marriages and health) as adults. Those who felt less favored have more physical and mental problems and poorer self-esteem; they tend to blame their siblings, rather than their parents, for the disparity.

⁜

One reason that psychoanalysts are finally noticing siblings is that the focus in the field has shifted from intrapsychic processes to interpersonal transactions.* This less hierarchical, more egalitarian approach to theory and therapy naturally brings peer relations to the fore. And since siblings are the template for all peer relationships—even, some researchers say, for only children, for whom relatives or playmates serve as substitutes—sibling dynamics and dysfunctions suddenly loom large.

There is plenty to see once you start looking.** The phenomenon of childhood sibling rivalry, which, along with extreme favoritism, is the major contributor to sibling strife when mismanaged, has been recognized for years—the term first appeared in 1939—but only now can its implications for adults, and the critical role parents play in its outcome, be fully appreciated.

Brothers and sisters provoke the most intense, primitive aggression from the moment we meet them, long before we can love them. One friend of mine tried to persuade her mother to leave her baby sister on the bus, another remembers thinking how simple and delightful it would be to pitch

---

* As of 1980, there had been only two presentations about siblings at psychoanalytic meetings and not many more for the rest of the century. Since 2000, there have been at least ten.

** Much of the early research on siblings was on the effects of birth order, but since little consistent has come of this, and nothing that illuminates sibling strife, I omit it here.

his infant brother out the fourth-floor window, and a third recalls blanketing the entire interior of her newborn brother's crib—and smothering its sleeping occupant—with talcum powder. The fates of these would-be infanticides and their intended victims varied dramatically: The first are best friends, the second are distant but cordial, and the third are civil but fundamentally alienated. The contrasting (and, happily, non-fatal) outcomes depended on the atmosphere in the culprits' families even more than on their personalities.* People tend to attribute estrangement to personal disparities ("My sister and I have nothing in common," they say), which seems compelling but cannot be the whole truth. Rivalry never calcifies into serious, lasting alienation or antagonism without parental participation (which includes looking the other way); otherwise there would be no loving bonds among brothers and sisters with different temperaments, talents, and ways of life.

Ferocious competition among child rivals is perfectly normal. But worried parents, when they witness it, become siblings themselves all over again, reenacting every unresolved conflict from their youth. They ignore, overreact, distort, suppress, exacerbate, and take sides in their children's self-assertion battles, all the while thinking that their own conduct is either rational or impartial. The principal weapons they use to quell its fury are denial—"My son will have no problem accepting his baby sister because we explained that we were having her for

---

* Contemporary "blended" families provide occasions for sibling rivalry all over again when a remarried parent lavishes attention on a new baby young enough to be the older siblings' own child.

his sake," an expectant father I know confidently predicted—or the desperate advice-seeking that fuels the market for books with titles like *Siblings Without Rivalry*.

The most effective strategy is the most elusive: self-knowledge and empathy for all combatants.* Using this approach might have prevented a cousin of mine, whose much younger sister had been the outrageously preferred one, from cordoning off her own teenage daughter's room with a dog gate so that she would not be bothered by her toddler sister, and then taking no action when the older girl hid all the little one's stuffed animals inside. Bitter child rivals like these have the worst adult relationships of any siblings; they are often estranged for life.

In contrast, another family's memorable solution to brotherly hate was recalled admiringly at age seventy-five by the younger son, who had been the main instigator. Forceful and aggressive even as a child—he grew up to be a Broadway producer—he tormented his more pacific elder brother (a businessman-to-be), whose age-related privileges he resented. The eight-year-old threw toy trains at his ten-year-old victim's head, tossed his brother's favorite ball onto the roof, and removed the ladder when its owner scrambled up to retrieve it. Finally, in desperation, their parents took direct action: They hired a friend of theirs who was an amateur boxer to give the boys lessons. Duking it out in their child-sized gloves under his tutelage evened the odds for the more passive one and allowed both fighters to express their hostility safely and non-

---

* Self-knowledge involves identifying parent-fueled sibling strife in one's own history—envy, failures, unfair victories, and defeats.

punitively in a skilled, stylized format. After the battling brothers took the gloves off—and a few years elapsed—they became loving companions for the rest of their lives.

Not every family has access to a boxing teacher, but what really made these enemies into friends was their parents' intelligent involvement. They neither took sides nor ignored the violence; they defanged it.

How do adults find the wisdom to navigate their children's mutual wrath or resist the temptation to play favorites—the chief contributors to sibling strife? Best equipped are those who were well loved themselves (or who understand why they weren't) and who, like the biblical Esau and Joseph, have satisfying lives. Addressing unfinished business with one's own siblings is the best way to foster mutuality in the next generation.

Paradoxically, it is often parents' good intention to treat their children equally that paves the way to sibling hell. Equal distribution of love, always a myth, is a false leveler that cheats all recipients out of being appreciated for their unique qualities. An identical twin recalls his father proudly reporting to a family friend that he had always treated his sons with scrupulous evenhandedness when they were growing up. "There is such a thing as fifty-fifty," the father insisted. "And yet," the friend observed astutely, "you named the elder twin after yourself, and your wife named the 'baby,' who was two minutes younger, for her father." The sons' fates belied the father's claim. "More was always expected of me as the eldest," said the museum curator who had been his father's favorite from the very first and had the more successful career than his baby brother, who had been under investigation for shady real estate deal-ings. Deeply identified with his father, a respected judge, the elder twin became a father surrogate for his younger brother, bailing him out for life. But when their mother was dying and cognitively impaired, it was only "her" chosen son whom she was able to recognize. The old alliances never ended.

Parents are responsible for converting sibling rivalry into sibling strife in the first place, but it is the siblings themselves who perpetuate it. A sibling's life—or our fantasy about that life—continues to be the standard against which our own is measured.* Even when they are adults—even when their par-ents are dead—many siblings nurse memories of slights, re-calling to their detriment who was preferred and who overlooked, as Anna Freud Bernays and my own brother did. The ferocity of that residual resentment, which is based on real but ancient hurts, can shock the object of it. A wealthy and prominent professor picked the occasion of their mother's fu-neral to present the evidence that his younger brother's success as a writer had meant more to her than his own solid but less spectacular achievements. "When I was cleaning out Mom's house, I found an entire closet filled with your articles and only a shoebox of my stuff," he announced bitterly, the dis-parity still rankling at age sixty. The preferred child can be just as entrenched in defending his "rights": "What was I supposed to do, un-write my books?" said the fifty-four-year-old brother

---

* This starts early; one-year-old children notice differences in parental treatment and by the age of three evaluate themselves in relation to their siblings.

with the copious memento-filled closet. Envy and guilt can make dialogue seem impossible, even pointless.

Children in a family do not choose one another, any more than they select their parents or their parents' responses to them. The more we feel we were forced to be in our siblings' company, dragged down or unfairly compared to them through the years together, the more we want to flee when we can later on and find more suitable replacements; with considerable justice, those whose siblings disappoint or betray them say, "My friends are my family."

Yet it is a fantasy that we can excise our earliest companions from our inner world even if we eventually have nothing to do with them; we attempt to obliterate them at our peril.* I asked a thoughtful and accomplished man whether he reproduced any aspects of the relationship he had with his intrusive, envious, troubled younger brother, and his response was "No, no, no!" He protested too much. In fact, though he currently has many acquaintances and a busy social calendar, there is no real intimacy in his life. The brotherly bond continues to be his only, aversive, model; triply denying its power keeps him in its thrall.

Whenever families gather, siblings notoriously take up their accustomed positions and reproduce their original dynamics, as though the roles were etched on their brains, ready to be

---

* Since infant observation research shows that neonates perceive their siblings almost as early as their mothers and before they recognize their fathers, our siblings have been part of our psychic reality for a very long time and are unlikely to disappear from it.

magically reconstituted when the cast reassembles—and not only then. But other influences shape us when we leave home. We cannot blame rivalry and unfair treatment in childhood for the problems we face as adults without forfeiting control of our destiny. Over time, connections between brothers and sisters develop their own momentum independent of how their parents behaved, just as our personalities metamorphose as we mature. This can further estrange adult siblings but can also facilitate empathy between them. At last, we can have some say.

Although there is no denying that struggles with siblings have an involuntary component at the onset, we have more influence over their later manifestations than we realize; awareness and the will to change can override years of reenacting the past. Life often presents opportunities—marriage, children, illness or death of a parent, changes of fortune—for rapprochement. But in order to make use of them, we must recognize our own participation in what went awry with our siblings and separate out our parents' role in determining the form that interaction took in childhood from what is possible in later years when there is no longer an intermediary. We do not need our antagonist's cooperation to accomplish this difficult feat; he or she need not even be alive. All we need is consciousness.

Choosing to reengage with the sibling relationship removes it from psychic storage and puts us face to face with the other person, without the intervening parent, for the first time. A new perspective on the past opens before us. With work, luck, and good will, we can even repudiate Cain's legacy.

CHAPTER 3

THE DANGLING CONVERSATION

Why Siblings Can't Talk to Each Other

⚛

I. The Unbearable Heaviness of Thinking About Siblings

Interviewing siblings about their conflicted relationships—I talked to 60 of them, aged twenty-six to eighty-three—is like pulling teeth. They aren't much better at discussing their brothers and sisters than the boobies, the siblings in Genesis, or the Freud family. This surprised and disconcerted me since over the past twenty years I have conducted 240 interviews for books on other taboo topics, including one about life with physically disabled or seriously dysfunctional siblings. But in that case, the "normal" ones knew what their feelings were; they just had never felt free to express them. This time was different, even with people I had interviewed before.

There was nothing wrong with my subjects; it is the nature of sibling strife. Even those whose responses in any other context would be perceptive and self-aware simply cannot think straight when they try to describe what goes wrong in their interactions with their problematic siblings, let alone explain the origins of their difficulties. These interviews were long, and insights came only in the last few minutes. Many people said that the experience felt more like a therapy session than an interview. They made connections and had breakthroughs in understanding that had never happened in therapy—mostly because the topic had never come up.

Their accounts, with few exceptions, started out confused, rambling, tangential. I got lots of external details but very little sense of what was actually going on. Descriptions of conversations had a tip-of-the-iceberg quality and required elaborate explanations to make any sense. The profusion of irrelevancies indicated that siblings do not digest their experience of one another. There is no vocabulary to describe it—probably because the origins of their conflicts are old and obscure, even preverbal. As a result, a much larger than usual number of my questions (such as "Do you reproduce the dynamics between you and your sibling with other people in your life?") were answered with a dismissive, unexamined "no" or "I don't know."

Far more often than people in any other strained relationship, siblings really do not know why their bonds are broken and have no clue how to approach fixing them, even if they long to. Psychological sophistication is little help; quite a few excellent therapists are included among the brain- and tongue-tied. No other topic I have written about, including death of a parent, is so hard to address.

Sibling fog is also contagious, and I caught it. Attempting to fathom my subjects' experience and comprehend what was going on under the surface felt like struggling through quicksand, even after years of specializing in psychotherapy with siblings and trying to understand my relationship with my own brother. But the effort paid off, for interviewees and interviewer alike.

⚜

Sibling strife is far more pervasive than I imagined, and since people rarely discuss it outside the family, there is no consensus about how to address the problem. It festers, but outsiders never know; everybody thinks everybody else's relationships are amicable and Hallmark-close, even though evidence says otherwise. Admitting the truth about their own situation makes strife-ridden siblings feel hopeless as well as secretly ashamed and guilty; anyone who does not like a troublesome brother or sister or who feels uneasy about endlessly providing financial assistance or one-way emotional support feels like a "bad" sibling, which is akin to feeling like you have failed as a parent. I recently encountered a restaurateur I had interviewed about his chronically broke, out-of-control sister.

"She's finally admitted to our mother that she's an alcoholic," he told me—immediately adding sotto voce, "I wonder if I have anything to do with it."

As each of the interviews progressed, the fog started to lift for both participants. When distressed siblings find the courage to face their predicament and put denial and rationalization aside, they cannot stop talking. Under their defensive carapace is unhealed pain that can emerge unexpectedly; I witnessed a crusty, self-possessed, eighty-three-year-old psychiatrist burst into tears of self-recrimination, regret, and love regained as he described his deathbed reconciliation with the sister he had fallen out with twenty-five years ago and had not seen or spoken to since.

When people I knew discovered that I was writing about this topic, they, too, suddenly felt license to tell their stories. Only then did I learn that a close friend's husband, my exercise coach, and my husband's best friend had all been cheated out of inheritances by siblings, with their parents' implicit or explicit compliance—the first out of $50 million, the second out of a $500 legacy, and the third out of the family home he had helped build. Siblings have a lot to say, and a lot to feel, when they let down their defenses.

II. Sibspeak: Sibling Conversation and Its Discontents

Strife-ridden siblings have a morbid fear of the telephone. To them, it is not an innocuous communication device, but a weapon and an instrument of torture. Thank God for Caller

ID! At any moment, when you are least expecting it, your sibling could call. And if you don't get a call, you feel obligated to make one. You cannot wait to get off the phone and at the same time feel compelled to be on it—at least on birthdays and holidays.

There is a special language used by estranged siblings both on the phone and in person that I call Sibspeak. On the surface, it sounds like English, but it has a grammar and vocabulary all its own. Its purpose, unlike ordinary language, has nothing to do with conveying information. Sibspeakers rarely say what they mean. Beneath the labored talk about the weather, sports, children, and politics (only a safe topic if you agree) is the real agenda: discharging obligations, reciting grievances, endless and futile attempts to "fix" the other person. Buried emotions—anger, anxiety, guilt, feelings of abandonment, resentment, or even repulsion—are always lurking, conveyed primarily by inflection. No matter what these siblings seem to be talking about, the real topic of "conversation" is the problematic relationship that they bend over backward to avoid facing. The truth never gets brought up; nobody ever says, "Why are you always angry at me?" or "Don't you want anything but money?" or "I feel bad that all we can talk about is the weather." A writer whose relationship with his elder brother had devolved into polite inanities concealing old conflicts told me, "What I really want to tell him is 'You used to be my interesting older brother and you're not anymore. What happened? Why did you change? What did I have to do with it?'"—but he knows this conversation will never take place.

In Sibspeak, good intentions go awry. The check-in call, which friendly brothers and sisters enjoy making so they can hear the sound of the other one's voice, has the opposite effect for siblings locked in combat. They feel helpless as the conversation inevitably morphs into a walk on eggshells. Yet they seem hypnotized, never objecting or confronting their interlocutors. There is a numbingly repetitive, even compulsive, quality about these exchanges.

A social worker who always tries to mend fences with her ailing, envious younger sister, described a typical conversation: "I call her all the time because she's going through medical problems, and there's always an angry person on the other end of the line. If I don't say something just right, it'll blow up. I get off the phone and wonder why did I just call her? It never goes anywhere. I don't get anything back, but I keep calling."

Another sister, the more solvent and successful of two siblings, reports an eerily similar deadlock. She feels that she cannot connect with the embittered one no matter how hard she tries: "I talk to her for thirty minutes, and when I finally tell her I need to go, she always says, 'You never have time for me,' and slams down the phone. Naturally I'm always the one who picks it up again. But once I didn't call her back for three weeks. She thought she was punishing me for not calling herself, but I felt a great relief."

When I asked her why she put up with such rudeness, she answered, "Guilt. She's blood, and I got things she didn't get." Her need to compensate for having a better life keeps her locked in an unwinnable pattern; she can never even the score or do her sister any good.

Sibspeak is the ideal medium for expressing passive-aggressive tendencies. A brother drives his sister crazy because "he talks really, really s-l-o-w-l-y, and he rambles, and I have to come up with excuses to get off the phone." But does she ever say, "I think something's going on between us because our conversations are so strained. I have a feeling you probably don't talk so slowly when you speak to anybody but me. What gives?" Directness is verboten in Sibspeak.

A nurse cannot stand her sister's clinging monologues. "She calls and says, 'I just want to ask you a question,' and an hour later she's still on the phone," she told me with resentful resignation. But it takes two to prolong such misery. If she realized there was no way to avoid offending her sister, she could terminate the endless interrogation.

Aggressive-aggressive tendencies are also easy to express in this peculiar tongue. A man resents the fact that his older brother, with whom their elderly mother lives in another state, never simply requests that he visit. "He'll command me rather than ask me, and say, 'Get down here and see your mother,' as though I'm neglecting her," he complained to me, but not to his self-appointed conscience. Out of the blue, a woman announced to her younger sister, "You were a horrible child. You cried all the time." The former crybaby could not say a word. "Sam and I are drinking again and loving it!" a party girl said gleefully to the responsible older sister who always bailed her out. The recipient of this charming announcement held her tongue, instead of telling the tipsy one to keep her alcohol consumption to herself since she clearly had no intention of doing anything about it.

My subjects reported the following conversation-stopping comments by siblings that took them off-guard, none of which was really about the overt content:

> "You embezzled the money I contributed to Dad's birth-
> day present."
> "I'm never coming to your house again because the last
> time I was there, you made me go outside to smoke."
> "You never thanked me for the flowers I gave you in 1982."
> "Mother told me she wanted me to have all her jewelry."
> "I'm afraid when our parents die that you'll take every-
> thing and not leave anything for me."

Any of these remarks could be defanged or contained by addressing, rather than ignoring, their hostile intent.

Limiting the interaction is sometimes the only way to stem the tide of Sibspeak. A psychotherapist repeatedly finds herself working for free when she talks to her difficult sister, whom she calls only out of obligation and as infrequently as she can. "In these conversations she spends most of the time telling me about catastrophic problems in her life. Our parents made her go to therapy a couple of times, but she quit, and now she openly says, 'You're my therapist.' I change the subject, but when I confront her, she gets angry and defensive. Then she'll call back and make efforts to inquire about my life, but I never want to tell her a thing."

The dutiful social worker who regularly calls her perennially aggrieved sister needs to master the art of sibling management on the rare occasions when her sister actually calls her. "She phones me maybe every three months," she told me. "I'm happy when she does, but then she'll say, 'I haven't heard from you,' and I don't know what to do then." I suggest taking charge by saying, "Why bring that up? We're talking now—let's make the most of it." This approach seemed novel and liberating to her.

Many beleaguered siblings described a pseudo-conversational gambit that speaks volumes, one that I experienced repeatedly with my own brother: the plaintive "Will I ever see you again after Mom dies?" Now I recognize the accusation—as well as the pain—at the heart of this question; he was really saying, "You're a bad, neglectful sister, and I mean nothing to you." In hindsight, rather than squirming inwardly and ignoring him, I should have replied, "Would you really want to see me? If so, rather than just accusing me of neglect or feeling lousy about it, let's work on our relationship so we want to be together." Translating Sibspeak into plain English might have broken the spell.

Guilty achievers naturally adopt Sibspeak when they address their less successful kin. They turn into motivational speakers or cheerleaders who try to influence the behavior of their audience or show them the error of their ways, strategies guaranteed to accomplish nothing but resentment. "Get happier," the businessman says to his depressed sister, as though this exhortation would make any difference. This is the same as telling an obese person to "lose weight," and induces the same rage and helplessness. Like worried, clueless parents trying to motivate their children to do better in school by chiding them, they fail to empathize or see the futility of such a strategy. Becoming a sibling's life coach always backfires.

After we spoke, the unwilling sister/therapist did in fact become aware of how she treated her "patient" and felt both chagrin and sadness when she recognized the condescension that pervaded her every word: "My sister and I are having dinner, and she says, 'I'm thinking of painting my kitchen the color of the vest you're wearing'—so of course a vision of where she's living, which is a disaster, comes to mind. I say, 'Audrey, I think you should paint it a warmer shade than this—the place needs some cheer. I really don't think your choice is a good idea.' I'm so bossy, controlling, and dominant with her; I'd never talk that way to a friend. Whenever I'm with her, I feel a tightening and protectiveness in my body. I don't want to get into anything difficult, but it always seems to happen."

Much of the paralysis siblings feel when they try to communicate is actually evasive action. Their anxiety to avoid the showdown, the blowup, the final estrangement and loss keeps them in a rut phone call after phone call, year after year. They never even imagine that there could be an alternative course of action.

But at the deepest level, the problem you have in communicating with a difficult brother or sister (the "tightening" and "protectiveness in my body" that the therapist so eloquently describes) is not interpersonal. It is the unwillingness to communicate with yourself about the relationship. Anxiety about knowing and revealing unacceptable feelings inhibits what you say to the other person. The terminal awkwardness of these conversations comes from a fantasy that by avoiding discussing "anything difficult," you can prevent siblings from knowing the awful truth—a truth they actually already know and feel themselves.

⁂

Adept Sibspeakers do not have to employ words to convey their thoughts or even address themselves directly to their victims. Their emotions are often deflected onto substitutes— children or spouses of siblings, parents, current events, gay rights, even home furnishings; two sisters stopped talking when one gave away the curtains the other had bought her and had not informed the giver that she was redecorating. The old battles are fought over all sorts of obscure things.

A financial advisor whose relationship with her younger brother had been marred for years by covert competition and hostility received an overtly congratulatory call from him after her second child was born. "He called me unexpectedly while I was in the hospital—if I had had Caller ID, I would never have answered the phone. Even as he was congratulating me, I could feel the competitive stuff coming out. Then he asked, 'Does Max love his baby brother?' What was

I supposed to say? Of course he doesn't yet. I wondered whether he was setting me up; my brother's always been all about marketing. I just wanted to get off the phone as quickly as possible."

Politics, that common bone of contention even between people who like each other, provides the perfect vehicle for sibling hostility masked as principle, as a conservative music teacher who had never gotten along with her left-leaning sister discovered during an election campaign: "My sister is extremely liberal, and I'm on the right. When Sarah Palin was nominated for vice president, I thought she'd have a fit. She berated me constantly, and when I wanted to drop it, she stopped talking to me—she's so rigid that she can't tolerate our differences. I can talk to other liberals, but she wants me to explain why I am the way I am. It's really about my being different from her. When the Democrats won Congress, I had to get on board. She started yelling at me, shouting that all the conservative siblings of her friends have come over to her side. It shook me. I expected her to listen to me; it hurt that it never happened about that or anything else." A lifetime of psychological insensitivity and unresolved clashes that may actually be mutual is the problem in this family, not political differences.

Sibspeakers can be blissfully unaware that they are not speaking English and then feel like the injured party when their siblings are offended by the attitudes they convey. A lighting designer was baffled that her sister, who had been in a lesbian relationship for twenty-five years, perennially rejected her overtures. "This is very close to my heart," she said, with genuine distress. "You've grown up with this person, and you don't understand what's going on. Now it's a polite standoff—but when we lived closer we had a compatible relationship." As she described her efforts to bridge the gap between them (and succumbed to the geographical-proximity fallacy), it was clear that she was giving her sister a very different message than she thought she was. "As soon as she announced she was a lesbian, my position as her sister became secondary. I said, 'You're a lesbian first and a sister second,' and she had nothing to say. She can't override whatever her lifestyle leads her to think or feel and look happily upon her sister."

It was her sister's sexual politics, she insisted, that had created such an unbridgeable gap between them. "She's very liberal and associates mostly with lesbian friends. I never said anything against her except that I don't believe there should be gays in the military." To demonstrate how far she bent over to be tolerant, she added, "My husband and I have even accepted her partner—she's like a member of the family." I asked whether she had the same attitude toward her other sister's husband. "But he *is* a member of the family," she protested. She was especially pained that her gay sister had spurned her by not inviting her to the wedding: "She wanted me to congratulate her on her marriage and I said 'I can't do that,'" she insisted, not seeing how provocative and rejecting her refusal must have felt to the couple. It was impossible for her to grasp that it was she herself who could not look happily on someone with a different life.

Although siblings can lapse into their strange, special language at any time, holidays and other family occasions are rife with it; the forced togetherness aggravates all the old, unresolved grievances.

A scatter-brained teacher told me in minute detail about a bruising conversation with her more organized sister that I found almost impossible to comprehend. They were ostensibly discussing where to hold a baby shower for the teacher's daughter, but the conversation rapidly disintegrated into a bitter mutual grievance recital. Her sister suggested holding the event in New York, where most of the family lived, but the grandmother-to-be claimed that her daughter wanted it in Vermont. The sister countered with a suggestion to hold two showers, one in each location, to accommodate everybody, but the mother of the guest of honor said her daughter didn't want to travel. "I said, 'Let's just have it in Vermont,' and she was furious. She said, 'I feel completely ditched. I've got to go to Boston for my son's concert that weekend, and you just said this is how you're gonna do it. I really don't want to travel with mother for hours in the car to get there.' I felt really selfish, but I didn't want to take her call to discuss it anymore."

In the welter of details she provided (that her daughter had just moved back from California to Vermont, that her sister, who was more organized, was generally judgmental of her because her life was more chaotic), I was struck by the mutual deafness of these two. The celebrant's aunt seemed not to consider the pregnant woman's convenience at all, preoccupied as she was with her sister's inconsiderateness. The mother-to-be's mother, on the other hand, never acknowledged to her sister that she was changing the established plans, nor did she take seriously her sister's discomfort about being stuck driving their mother, with whom she had a contentious relationship. When I asked my subject what she really thought was going on, she said with sorrowful ferocity, "My sister hates me, and she doesn't want to admit it to herself or anybody else"; she was no doubt unconsciously talking about her own feelings as well. "I feel like I've been bugging her for her entire life—just by being born." That sentiment, I thought, would be a place to start a real conversation, in plain English.

But the Big Two, Thanksgiving and Hanukkah/Christmas, really bring out the nonstop Sibspeak; these are the times that fantasies of family harmony (and the realities of family cacophony) compel us the most. Every detail of holiday planning and execution—location, gifts, attendance, activities—is dangerous terrain, rife with possibilities for misunderstanding.

Who will host the family gathering is often the pretext for a repeat performance of a very old battle. In one family, two sisters reenact their rivalry yearly over this burning question. The more complacent of the two says, "I tell her we're going to have Thanksgiving at my house and she says, 'Stop right there. *I'm* going to make the dinner and *you're* invited.' I say that my children may be coming, and she says, 'When will you know for sure?' When I say that I'll know two weeks beforehand, she says, judging me as usual, 'You're at this point in your life, and you still can't make a decision.' She's brutal. I try to challenge her and she says, 'I feel like you're scolding me, and I don't like it.' And then I give up."

One wonders how many times they have had this argument, the various forms it has taken over the years, and why it must be perennially revisited—questions both of them are far too involved in their struggle to contemplate. It never occurs to either of them to simply alternate venues.

Discussing Thanksgiving plans with an unhappy, envious sibling is awkward and guilt inducing, particularly when you are closer to your parents than she is. Being aware of the discrepancy doesn't make it any easier to navigate, as the therapist who is her troubled sister's unwilling advisor described: "Even though I try not to talk about our parents, the topic came up, and I said that they wanted to go out for Thanksgiving dinner. She says, 'I think they don't like being in my house,' which is true. Then she says, 'I'm happy because now I can just show up and not have to bring a dish,' but then she adds, 'Of course nobody consulted me—nobody ever does because I'm the single one.' I know that's not the real reason; it's her general incompetence. I didn't say, 'Oh gosh, I should have talked to you,' because it would be a lie—her life is a disaster, and I would never consult her about anything. If she was different, I would have discussed it with her, but I didn't want to get into it."

I asked this thoughtful woman why it was impossible for her to make any real contact with her sister despite the obstacles— after all, she had surely dealt with defended and difficult people in her life before. "Whenever I try, it's only explosive. Both of us say things we wish we hadn't," she explained. "We just can't seem to talk." Then she made an observation that boded well: "I also don't believe I've taken the time to find a way to reach her." When I wondered why not, she said, "It feels like a gigantic piece of work. I have a son with ADHD, my marriage is challenging because I grew up in a troubled one, and I work full-time; my plate's really full—I have to deal with what's right in front of me." I observed that dealing with a problem sibling always gets shoved to the sidelines, and she took it in. "I'm hearing myself say there's not room in my life to do this, as though there's just a finite amount of room." This insight, if she pursues it, could ultimately make a difference in how she talks to her sister and how she feels about herself.

Self-aware siblings do not want to slip into Sibspeak every time they address their adversaries, but to their dismay they find that they do so anyway. A high school principal succumbed when she made an obligatory birthday phone call to her younger brother, who is the black sheep of their large, closely entwined family and a particular vexation for her. Despite her best efforts, she got caught up in the compelling manifest content of their conversation and in her long-standing role as his critic, which prevented her from perceiving the hurt beneath his words. "I called him on his birthday and all he talked about is the plans for Christmas," she said contemptuously, not noticing that he might not have known what else to say or that he might have felt a need to deliver news he knew she wouldn't want to hear as quickly as possible to get it over with. "He said he was only coming for the last two days, and I said, chidingly, 'You ought to come for the whole time.'"

I observed that her brother's discomfort with his outsider status might have prompted him to truncate his visit, a fact she might not want to recognize because she was part of the problem. I suggested that she might try addressing his feelings instead of criticizing him for having them by saying something like "It must be tough to come to these family gatherings. You never feel like you're part of things, and you know that I am." "But wouldn't that be rubbing salt in the wound?" she asked. I responded that acknowledging his legitimate discomfort would be more empathic than insisting he come when he would be miserable. It might not work, but there was a chance that it might make him feel better understood and lessen the gap between them. What did she have to lose? "I have the gift for doing what's worst," she said, blaming herself for her blindness. Acknowledging that "gift," which every strife-ridden sibling possesses, is the first step to stopping the incessant, numbing, and painful flow of Sibspeak.

CHAPTER 4

THE BANK OF BRO AND SIS

Siblings Who Sponge

⁂

Manny Hernandez still has the sculpted cheekbones, taut physique, and Latin glamour that made him a sought-after model in his youth. Now in his early fifties, with a picture-perfect wife and family, he owns several popular restaurants in Miami. But his obese, alcoholic sister, who cannot make a living or maintain a relationship, haunts him. She tugs at his purse strings as much as his heartstrings. He feels used but cannot say no.

Of all the topics that divide siblings, money is right up there with parental favoritism; in fact, the two issues are often related. The preferred sibling is also usually the more successful one, and with that success comes guilt and a heightened sense of responsibility. Money is the most obvious way to assuage the guilt and discharge the responsibility.

Siblings who sponge—or whose inclination to do so has to be held in check—torment their more solvent brothers and sisters with their ever-changing, often implicit, demands. They are a different breed from siblings in temporary need because of illness or accidents of fortune, who appreciate and reciprocate financial assistance in a crisis; for them money is part of a loving bond that draws the pair closer. But the chronically entitled are never grateful, even when they are desperate.

The combination of emotional connection, responsibility, resentment, and there-but-for-fate-go-I anxiety makes many higher-functioning siblings vulnerable to emotional blackmail. What, they worry, will happen to her children if I don't cough up? Where will he live if I won't cosign the lease? If our parents die or cannot continue supporting him, do I have to step in—what about my own family and my future, let alone my inheritance? Visions of seeing your sister begging in front of the church where you both went to Sunday school (which actually happened to one subject of mine) or finding your brother on your doorstep one night (a perennial fear of another) haunt them. And the problem sibling does not have to be severely disabled to provoke these fears, only perennially dependent on family subsidies for whatever reason.

Some beleaguered siblings put their foot down on principle and refuse to give any financial aid, as I did; after one too many requests, I finally wrote my brother that "the only thing I cannot give you is money." Others are the proverbial soft touch, even though they kick themselves afterward and their spouses get mad. To guarantee a sibling's well-being can seem like a duty, particularly when aging parents reinforce this conviction;

"Look after your sister" is a disturbingly common deathbed request. Sibling caretaking, a task that has often been assigned since childhood, then becomes a lifetime responsibility.

Overt family pressure to provide loans with no due date is even more formidable when it augments the internal pressure to do so. But yielding reflexively without considering the toll (or the likely efficacy) can convert your business into a sheltered workshop and your professional success into a private foundation for a beneficiary not entirely of your choosing. Whatever course you follow, a struggling sibling cannot fail to haunt you.

Responsibility for a sibling's welfare rarely stops with cold cash. Help can take a variety of forms, like underwriting therapy for a niece whose husband mistreats her or offering tuition to a favorite nephew who is academically gifted. But such support is seldom accepted with thanks; the niece's mother thought her sister was meddling, and the parents of the scholarship recipient expected one for each of their children. Acts of generosity are usually taken for granted, which spares the recipient shame for needing them. Whether the "gift" is a $25,000 down payment on a condo or a $600 plane ticket home (each of which subjects provided for their siblings), the compulsiveness of the donor is directly related to the insouciance of the recipient. Helping out morphs into enabling, motivated not by altruism or necessity, but by the need to assuage one's conscience for having a better life or to maintain a family tie at any price.

⁜

Manny and his sister, Celia, were army brats whose nomadic childhoods caused them to rely on each other for companionship early on. But the trajectories of their lives had diverged radically by the time they were teenagers. Manny became an Eagle Scout, then an athlete, and then, with his mother's encouragement ("She always saw a drive in me," he observed), embarked on the modeling career that made him a fixture in magazines and on runways worldwide.

Meanwhile, Celia, who was two and a half years younger, "went with the bad kids and was always in a little bit of trouble," according to her brother. She eventually dropped out of high school and ended up a divorced single mother who worked in a health food store and couldn't make ends meet without her brother's help. "She had talents," Manny said wistfully, "but she got trapped in the wrong direction. I was Mr. Goody Two Shoes, the golden boy who could never do anything wrong, while she was always on the verge of breaking down." He knows he was the favorite, the bearer of his mother's aspirations.

Manny spoke of Celia with a mixture of pain and defensiveness. "She thought things fell into my lap and that I got stuff through the way I looked. But I worked hard and managed to make a lot of money." Manny invested in a little Cuban restaurant in South Beach, which has grown into a chain of three fashionable nightspots and made him a fortune. He also married a singer, entered the real estate market, and now has three children and an enviable life.

Celia never thinks twice about turning to Manny for emotional as well as material aid, which he gives guiltily and sometimes grudgingly. "I testified in her divorce, helped raise her son, and put a roof over her head," he said with some rancor. But when he sold the building in which he had given her a discounted apartment and made her then-husband property manager, she stopped talking to him for two years—a typical response to a gift that becomes an entitlement.

Manny described the dilemma that many successful people with a dysfunctional sibling, even one who has no serious disability, struggle with. "I care, but I don't care—it's a weird thing," he confessed. "She makes me uncomfortable; it's hard to relate to her. I always think I'm stealing her thunder. I'd like to get far away from her, but I feel horrible at the thought. I have such a small family—there are just the two of us. I don't want to be mean to her"—as if refusing to bail her out would constitute an act of hostility rather than an act of self-protection.

Manny took action, however ineffectual, when he saw Celia standing outside a bar "extremely drunk." "It worried me because there's alcoholism in our family and I warned her," he said, unintentionally fueling her envy and shame even more.

What drives Manny crazy is that Celia makes no efforts to straighten out her life, and he fears he will be stuck with the job forever. "I don't want to take care of her, but I have an obligation. She lets herself go—now she's dating a bartender. I try to set her up to be happy; if she weren't so needy or angry our relationship would be better." He weeps in sorrow and frustration, caught between pity, anxiety, and resentment at being manipulated. Even if she never heeds his exhortations, he "just can't cut her off."

The more prosperous you are, the more difficult it is to justify not providing for a struggling sibling, especially if you feel that you have been favored over that sibling by your parents or by luck. Providing financial aid is often motivated by an unconscious need to compensate for what seems like an unfair advantage that can never be righted. Once siblings acknowledge these feelings, their futile, even harmful attempts to undo a fait accompli can cease, and their efforts on a sibling's behalf become more circumspect.

Dr. Warren Franklin was his physician-father's designated heir from birth; he was named for a famous neurologist. Of the three sons, he alone was invited to accompany his father on house calls as a child, a distinction he remembers to this day. Now he is a noted sixty-five-year-old neurologist in Beverley Hills, the only one of his siblings to enjoy professional and financial success.

Warren, who keeps a distance from both of them, is particularly embarrassed and tormented by his youngest brother, Michael, who, despite his intelligence, has never married or held a steady job. But when Michael recently had a massive heart attack and ignored his doctor's orders, his self-destructive behavior was excruciating for Warren to witness both as a brother and as a physician; he had to get involved. "Of course, he has no insurance and doesn't take care of himself," Warren told me with a mixture of concern and contempt. "I can't stand to be connected with him, but I went to his shack—he lives in a trailer-thing—to try to help him." Even though Michael rebuffed his brother's efforts to arrange medical care and never picks up the phone when he calls, Warren irrationally blames himself for Michael's desperate situation, as though his money could have magically transformed his brother's destiny and mended the emotional damage. "I feel intensely guilty that I've let his life come to this. I'd feel terrible if he died," he admitted.

Warren feels so responsible for his brother that he is considering selling a valuable piece of property that is a major part of his parents' estate, of which he is executor. "Maybe I should, maybe I'm supposed to, just sell it all and give him the money," he repeated several times during our talk. His internal struggle blinds him to the reality that such an action would disregard the rights of the other siblings and is unlikely to change a lifetime of neglect. He ruminates over his impossible choices, hoping to assuage his conscience by a dramatic financial gesture, torn between feeling compelled to be his brother's keeper and wanting to run the other way.

Not every caretaker sibling feels the punishing ambivalence that troubles Manny and Warren, but most are peeved by the recipient's ingratitude, even if they never doubt their mission as the family savior. Susan Edwards, a sixty-year-old lawyer and the eldest of four sisters, believes unquestioningly that assisting her erratic youngest sister is her duty, as though she herself were the parent. She grew up in that role, her dying father reinforced her conviction by asking her to do so in perpetuity, and her marriage to the heir to a large fortune made it possible. Still, she is acutely aware that her efforts, while they have clearly had some positive effects, have inadvertently sown envy as well as dependency and have done nothing to improve her sister's self-esteem. Even though she sees that her largesse only reinforces the gulf between their lives, she would never think of curtailing it. "I sense a constant slight criticism of me," Susan observed with characteristic understatement. "When I got a new car with air conditioning she said '*I've* never had an air-conditioned car,' and she said that I spend every summer in Maine. That's not true—they've always used our house," she added in her own defense, as though she needed to justify her advantages.

Susan's efforts on her sister's behalf go well beyond lending her a summer place. "When she got a job out of town, I invited her daughter to live with us, which she did for several years—I was like her surrogate mother. Then my sister really resented me; not only do I have a house in Maine, but I've got her daughter, too," she said, her bitter irony mingled with recognition.

Susan went on to pay for her niece's private school and, later, for her wedding party. "I was happy to do it," she said. She accepts the sniping as an unpleasant but unavoidable part of doing her duty, and she never confronts it. Tolerating bad treatment is the price she pays for her own good fortune.

⁂

You don't have to be wealthy, or even solvent, to feel torn about the fate of a wayward sibling. How much responsibility you are willing to assume for that fate is a subjective decision, based on temperament, family dynamics, and the meaning of the relationship.

Dana and Abby Turner, students in their mid-twenties with part-time jobs, have watched their thirty-four-year-old elder sister, Maggie, haplessly go through men, careers, and money as she has moved around the country for years. She comes home only when she is in dire straits and shows little interest in them the rest of the time. They simultaneously worry about her and resent that she thinks nothing of asking them for "loans," even though they both struggle to make ends meet. Dana, the youngest, finds her self-centered, "diva" sister compelling even though she recognizes her faults. Fear for Maggie's welfare as much as their personal bond—when Dana was a teenager, she idealized Maggie as an artistic free spirit—underlie her willingness to help. Abby, the more serious and realistic middle child, has disengaged. She and Maggie were never close, and her sister's insensitivity conflicts with her own values. One gives, the other doesn't.

Dana said, "As much as I recognize that Maggie can be a leech and a user, her fragility has always been close to the surface; it makes me feel like I am an assistant to her life. She's massively in debt and financially dependent on the family. I don't have much myself, but three months ago she asked to borrow a thousand dollars and I gave it to her. I'll never see it again." Dana has found a way to avoid being shamelessly exploited by her sister, at least for the present: "I'll figure out some way to make her pay it back, like staying with her on vacation and not giving her rent." She is willing to go through these machinations because, she admits, "I feel sad for her, and also scared for her."

Abby has had enough of her elder sister's irresponsibility and repudiates the role that Dana tolerates. "I've told my mother not to give her money," she said. "Maggie has an addictive personality, and no self-awareness; I won't be an enabler. It will be difficult for me not to contribute when our parents are gone, but I know it wouldn't help." Her conviction about the proper course of action protects her from the guilt that many siblings in her situation find inescapable.

Keeping a sibling afloat financially is not necessarily virtuous, nor is refusing to do so cold or cruel. Whether the person seems unwilling, or genuinely unable, to function as an independent adult is an important factor in the decision to help. But the most powerful (and usually unconscious) determinant is hope—hope that your money can make a lasting difference, hope that providing it will foster appreciation, neutralize envy, show your moral rectitude, or please your parents. Secretly you imagine, like Manny, that when your sibling becomes "less needy and less angry" because of your intervention, a real filial bond will suddenly be possible.

But hope does not always spring eternal; it is not always the best policy either. Hope can blind you to the real causes of a brother's or sister's predicament, of which financial woes are only a manifestation, and which may be beyond your power (or anybody's power) to amend. Buying health or happiness for another is rarely possible, and compulsive efforts to do so can damage your own.

The ways that siblings cope with the dilemma of whether or not to contribute run the gamut from steadfast refusal to unequivocal assent. There are some who, like Abby, never doubt that providing financial support does no lasting good and refuse to do it and others who come to this conclusion only when their repeated efforts lead nowhere. Withholding aid is never easy because it leaves you feeling like a helpless witness to your closest relative's pain, but it can be liberating.

Nancy Cameron, a forty-seven-year-old psychiatric nurse, has always insisted that she will not subsidize her forty-two-year-old sister, June, whose most recent job—she changes them frequently because she tends to get fired for insubordination—is working as a clerk in a pet store. "I refuse to help her now, and my plan is to continue to refuse after my parents die," Nancy said with strong conviction. "I'm angry that she doesn't take more responsibility financially or emotionally. My parents help her a lot—she's never bought her own car." Like many clear-sighted siblings, Nancy believes that her sister is capable of improving her lot and that her parents are doing June no favors by infantilizing her. Like

Dana and Abby, she is "scared that I might feel scared" about her decision if June deteriorates, but she stands firm because "It's the right way to do it." She had no difficulty telling her parents that "they have to figure out things financially" for her sister's future because "it's not my responsibility."

Getting burned is often the way a sibling learns to opt out. Sixty-seven-year-old high school teacher Larry Atkins once helped his gifted, self-destructive younger brother, Bob, in a crisis but soon discovered that one crisis only led to another, until Bob died last year at age sixty-four, weighing four hundred pounds and collecting welfare. "He always left messes for me to clean up," Larry recalled with anger and sorrow. "When he was a wreck, he came to live with me for a month, but then I had to tell him, 'You're in free fall, and you're not falling on me,' and it turned really ugly. I gave him money too, but at that point I said to him, 'I'm not going to do it anymore because that will keep you where you are.' It was awful to watch, but I had to learn to defend myself. Over time I got better at not letting him affect me." He never stopped loving his brother but refused to have his own life ruined by him.

The intervention of someone outside the family is a godsend for a sister who gives too much. Ruth Grant is the only one of her siblings who has a professional degree, and she has always been acutely aware of the discrepancy between her life and that of her three brothers, particularly her youngest and least functional one. When Teddy asks for help, she has always asked, "How much?" Finally, Teddy asked her to lend him $30,000. "I was planning to send him a check even though it meant that I couldn't pay back my student loans," she confessed. "Fortunately, my husband sets good limits and wouldn't let me do it. That ended my enabling crap." Ruth's husband granted her permission to end a pattern of behavior that she longed to stop but felt compelled to perpetuate.

With time and experience the relationship with needy siblings evolves in either direction; how they behave and what they do with your contributions make you reassess their character and the role you should take in their lives. But estrangement and accusations of selfishness are the painful consequences if you decide to withhold support.

Forty-two-year-old software designer Nick Adams used to help his thirty-nine-year-old sister, April, financially because he had been favored over her as a child and was much more prosperous as an adult; "I was the golden one in our family," he said. "I had a wake I was unaware of." April's personal and pecuniary troubles weighed on him, and at first he had tried to lighten them. But later on, he concluded that April was reckless rather than genuinely needy. "When she needed money as a single mom, I gave her two thousand dollars and told her not to pay it back, just to put it into her child's college fund, but when she asked for money again after skipping out of thousands of dollars of tolls, I told her she needed to repay me. Since that day I've been branded as cold and moneygrubbing. She felt that I'd never done enough for her; she could tell I was judging her for blowing off the tickets. Now we only see each other on family occasions, and it's awkward. I still love her and still want what's best for her—there's very little that I wouldn't do to help her if she wouldn't end up holding it against me." But he knows she cannot and keeps his distance.

Seeing how the recipient of your help treats somebody else can often give you a more objective perspective, making a victim seem more like a victimizer. Sympathy for her brother's plight kept forty-four-year-old foreign correspondent Wendy Jackson wiring him money from Istanbul for years, until observing how he exploited their aging father made her reconsider who he was and what she owed him.

Wendy and Richard, who is two years her senior, started out as close as Manny and Celia. Like Celia, Richard struggled in school. "He stuttered and was bullied," Wendy recalled. "His self-esteem was low from an early point. Some people get over it, but he never bounced back." By age twelve these "best pals" had little in common. "I was the normal kid who had friends and didn't stammer," she said, "and I knew I was going to college." As teenagers they both got summer jobs at a local restaurant, but their parents, in a misplaced effort to treat them equitably, made Wendy quit when Richard got fired.

Wendy appreciated her parents' genuine efforts on her brother's behalf—they gave him the money earmarked for his college education for the down payment on a house when it became evident he would not be attending—but like Nancy Cameron, she felt they "enabled him by being too soft"; their subsidies never carried any requirement that he make an attempt to become self-sufficient.

As time went on, Richard's life began to resemble "something out of Jerry Springer," a far cry from the experience of his sister and their "academically minded" family and one step away from welfare. "It was like when worlds collide," Wendy said. "He never managed his money or anything else." Richard drove taxis for twenty years, owned one for a while, and then lost it when he failed to make his loan payments on time. From then on he lived by selling off his collection of old cars and getting handouts from their parents. He was still asking for financial help into his fifties, even after his mother died and his father began to have health problems.

Two years ago Wendy decided to give Richard money to prevent his house from going into foreclosure. "I couldn't just sit around and not try to help because people sometimes get their act together," she explained. "I actually took out part of my own retirement fund because I didn't want to use my husband's family money." Richard took her money, proceeded to father a child, quit his job, and declare bankruptcy. Neither he nor his wife has made any attempt to work, let alone repay her. He is about to lose the house all over again.

This behavior registered with his sister. "I really feel clear about it now," she declared. "I saw I didn't make any difference." Richard had abdicated responsibility. "He could have made an effort; I did. I've been lucky, but life is both luck and what you work for." Her sympathy began to ebb with her diminished bank account.

But what really opened Wendy's eyes was the way that Richard continued to expect their aging and ailing father to

support him. "Now I'm just angry. He's a taker and a freeloader—
he's still sponging from our dad, who needs things himself now.
I'm more help from Istanbul than he is from down the street."
She vowed never to bail Richard out again.

⚛

When Larry Atkins, Ruth Grant, Nick Adams, and Wendy
Jackson learned through experience that giving money to their
brothers or sisters was a dead end that left them with little
besides regrets and emptier wallets, they cut off the cash flow,
although their concern for their relatives' fates continued. But
why do some siblings keep signing checks even when they see
that nothing changes and that they are exploited and insulted
in the bargain?

Sometimes all the awareness in the world that a sibling in
trouble is actually a user cannot make the one lending a helping hand withdraw it. Despite the evidence, these reluctant
benefactors keep giving because the lifeline goes both ways;
they are perpetuating the relationship for their own sake. For
them the need for family—to preserve personal history, to not
be alone in the world ("We're the only two left; she's all I've
got," they say)—runs deep, and they cling to it, even if they
have to pay for the privilege. Otherwise, all communication
and filial feeling could be lost, as happened to Nick. The suspicion that finances play a significant role in their relationship with their closest relatives is so disturbing that they

quickly bury it. Instead, they insist that they "adore" the sibling or list the person's fetching qualities (usually artistic or athletic ability) as justifications for continuing the subsidies. Siblings like these allow themselves to be mistreated, manipulated, and ignored without complaint for fear of losing the family bond and the image of themselves as good and generous people; they swallow their resentment and go back every time, checkbook in hand. They tolerate treatment from a sibling that would end marriages or friendships, that they would not accept from anyone else. No amount of ill use makes a lasting impression because it is the meaning of having of a sibling relationship, rather than its actual qualities, that they have to keep alive at any cost.

⁂

It is difficult to imagine that Nicole Cohen and her sister, Trish, come from the same planet, let alone the same family. Nicole, a thirty-four-year-old research librarian at an Ivy League university, dresses with prim simplicity and has a quietly intense and self-effacing, yet ironic manner. Her thirty-three-year-old sister is a flamboyant self-proclaimed loudmouth and cowgirl who books bawdy acts at a Reno nightclub and looks the part.

Even though she was eager to talk about the travails of their relationship, Nicole had trepidations about the impact of her revelations on her sister, whose feelings toward her are a constant source of anxiety. "If she sees this, I'm worried that she'd hate me even more, but it's my story too," she concluded, struggling to assert her right to her own point of view. As she told her story, a recital of humiliations that can only be described as sadomasochistic, it became clear that she feared her own hatred as much as her sister's.

Nicole's depiction of Trish's character and behavior was unsparing: "She's a charismatic, funny person, not as smart as me—I was classified as the scholarly one. She's a celebrity in her world, a self-focused firecracker who's completely insensitive and impossible to get along with. She lives chaotically in rural Nevada with her hunky husband. She's really mean to me but to others as well. I still find her behavior stunning, as familiar as I am with it."

Nicole admits that "it's a huge pain to get there, and I'm not sure I want to go," but she still dutifully visits her younger sister's family every year, bearing gifts and taking everyone out to dinner; these efforts are never reciprocated.

During the most recent trip, Trish "was in a vile mood the whole time, absolutely toxic." Nicole described a series of gratuitous insults and outrageous demands with which she dutifully complied, inwardly seething but never objecting. One morning, for instance, her sister asked her to clean the refrigerator. "While I was doing it, she calls her friends and tells them that I couldn't stand how dirty it was." The visitor said nothing (although of course it was true) and continued cleaning. Her hostess "never told me she was glad I had come. All she said when I left was 'I want to thank you for leaving the gas tank empty.' I knew that six days was too long to stay." Yet to truncate or skip a visit would seem perilous.

Although Nicole goes through the same punishing routine every time they see each other, she told me that she "felt so bad and so disappointed"—and then quickly added "I adore her," as if to neutralize the impact of revealing what she had endured. She also seemed unaware of what she conveys wordlessly to her sister and how her very presence and competence humiliate Trish, just as Michael Franklin, the uninsured cardiac patient who lives in the "trailer-thing," is offended by his physician brother Warren's attempts to help him.

Nicole's disappointment, which is her way of denying the ongoing degradations of their relationship, didn't stop after she got home. "My sister's husband called as if nothing had happened and asked for a fifteen thousand dollar loan for their house. I said, 'Trish wasn't even nice to me, and I had a horrible visit,' and he said, 'She'd be nice if you give us the money.'"

Only once did Nicole get mad at her sister to her face. "Trish doesn't play by the rules," she said. "She revealed a confidence to my mother even though I had kept the one she had entrusted to me. When I objected, she yelled, 'I'll tell her whatever I want' and hung up on me." Like an ill-disciplined child or pet, Trish suffered no consequences; Nicole was the one who called back. "We talk regularly. We've never had a falling out. I can't lose her," Nicole said passionately. Why does she take it?

A traumatic past, as well as the dynamics of the Cohen family, partially explain why she clings to her rebel sister ever more desperately the more abusive her behavior becomes. Orphans of divorced parents, their father died ten years ago six days after he was diagnosed with inoperable cancer, and left everything to his fiancée. Their mother has also since died. Even during their lifetimes, these parents clearly set no limits on Trish's behavior. Overwhelmed by her needs, they designated Nicole the responsible one and parent surrogate. "She's a black hole of attention," Nicole said. "I love her and still feel responsible for her, but I'm not sure why most of the time." There is a parental quality to the way she responds to her sister's usually well-concealed vulnerability. Nicole says, "I have access to parts of her that are like a little tiny child—when she cries it's terrible"; she does not say how her sister responds when she herself cries. She describes tending to Trish as "like taking care of this wild orchid—everything has to be in exactly the right daylight." "I adore her," added the reluctant horticulturist once more, with even more resolute intensity.

⁂

Nicole told me a dream about Trish that epitomizes the predicament of many compulsive caretaker siblings, one that contains a truth they refuse to recognize: "My sister was skiing with her kids, and she lost her cell phone. I kept trying to help her find it."

Despite the evidence, Nicole's dream shows how she clings to a delusion: if she not only retrieves but also pays for the "phone" (which represents maintaining connection and communication with her sister, who is always going "downhill"), they can have a genuinely reciprocal relationship. She keeps searching in order to keep hope alive because she cannot accept that Trish's phone will never be found. True sisterhood is not just a one-way collect call.

CHAPTER 5

A BROTHER IN THE BUSINESS

Sibling Strife at the Office

⚜

Ninety-five percent of businesses in the United States are family owned.* This means that the vast majority of America's workplaces, from the corner hardware store and the neighborhood coffee shop to the boardrooms of major corporations, are hotbeds of sibling strife—sometimes overt, more often doing damage underground. We already know that childhood conflicts are replicated in adulthood with latter-day representatives of the original players in the family drama. But what happens when those representatives are the actual figures from childhood, all grown up? Trouble lurks when you take your family to work. Every unresolved issue—rivalry, jealousy, envy, bitterly contested power differentials, the fallout from parents playing favorites—haunts siblings on the job not just on holidays but every weekday, all year round.

---

* Note: references for this chapter can be found on page 255.

Family businesses are also notorious for transferring pathology from one generation to the next, so that brothers and sisters who work together have to cope not only with their own disputes but also with detritus of ancient battles fought by their parents and grandparents with their own siblings. Since two out of five siblings described their adult relationships as "contentious" in a large study, it's a wonder any work gets done; it is an impressive achievement for harmony to reign when siblings labor side by side.

When the enterprise spans several generations, decisions that are bound to come up, such as succession and managerial hierarchy, easily reignite strife. Only one child can be anointed CEO-apparent, and that child is likely to be the one whom the parent/owners favored. Unless the one who is passed over has an independent professional identity—or excellent self-esteem—he or she can spend a lifetime nursing the wound.

A family has operated a historic hacienda hotel in the mountains of New Mexico for many decades. The current director was chosen over his older sister to run the operation two decades ago, and she has never forgotten it. They both live on the estate, but he occupies their parents' house. He honored the family tradition of providing for relatives by giving her a title and a stipend with few responsibilities. She sits on the advisory board, where her mission is to try to sabotage every proposal he presents, like adding a shop that sells their homemade chili specialties or expanding dining options to include a casual café in addition to the formal restaurant.

After both enterprises turned out to be popular and lucrative, she admitted that she had been wrong, which was a major breakthrough in their relationship. Constant diplomacy on his part and some mellowing on hers have decreased tensions over the years, but he still secretly hopes that she will decide to retire somewhere else.

The fallout from a family company often outlives the enterprise itself, continuing to plague siblings long after its founders are gone and the company is sold or liquidated. A hoard of expensive gold and diamond baubles was all that was left to the third-generation heirs of an ethnic foods corporation started by their immigrant grandfather and eventually sold to a national conglomerate by their parents, who had gone through much of the fortune. One sister, who was the favorite, locked the other (whom I interviewed) out of their mother's apartment right after she died and appropriated the loot. "Mother wanted me to have everything," she declared—and was later shocked and hurt when her sister wanted nothing more to do with her. "Let her talk to the jewelry," the disinherited one said bitterly.

Start-ups, too, are not immune to sibling stresses. Entrepreneurs whose businesses prosper are frequently lobbied by their relatives to employ their siblings and then have to deal with the consequences of either resisting or becoming the boss of their own closest relatives. However, if circumstances and personalities are propitious, this arrangement can actually work.

Two friends of mine, both of whom have older brothers, own restaurants around the block from each other—a hip all-night diner and a cozy Italian trattoria. One had the good fortune to hire his brother, and the other the wisdom not to. Ben, the diner owner, made his brother Steve, a genial, laid-back sixty-year-old former insurance agent, the night manager. Doug, the trattoria proprietor, resists constant family pressure to employ his elder brother, Joel, in any capacity.

Although Ben has two business partners, Steve is the only one of their siblings who works there. The lines of authority are clear and consciously designed to be so. Steve is a salaried employee but the one in charge on the graveyard shift. Friendly as children, the brothers respect and appreciate each other as adults ("He's my big brother, and I'll always think of him that way," Ben said), despite discrepancies in their life circumstances that could easily sow discord. Ben is a glamorous, married millionaire, and Steve is a divorced regular guy who is popular with customers and staff alike. Their working relationship mirrors their personal relationship, to the satisfaction and profit of both.

Doug's older brother, Joel, who is fifty-three, is much harder to take. He has brains and artistic talent but a personality so abrasive that he has alienated many employers, including Doug's identical twin, Seth, a jeweler who once yielded to parental pressure to employ Joel and lived to regret it. Like many a sibling in charge, Seth behaved like an overly lenient parent, putting up with too much and then blowing up. "Joel offended all Seth's customers," said Doug, "and I can't afford to let that happen to me, even though he keeps asking to work here." As a child, Joel was the odd one out, unable to compete with his more appealing younger brothers for their mother's attention, and the twins and he fought constantly, as they still do. But a sense of family solidarity obligates Doug to let Joel hang out at his restaurant, where he eats for free, brings his cronies, and constantly tries to pick up waitresses and single women patrons, behavior that infuriates his brother. Steve, on the other hand, has created a paternal role for himself. He considers the famously attractive staff at his brother's restaurant "like my daughters—they all tell me their problems." At Doug's place, Joel is the problem.

Siblings who fail to resolve their childhood rivalries make bad bosses and worse employees. A manager whose relationships with staff are strictly business can demand proper work habits and discipline personnel who break the rules, but with a brother or sister the boundaries are blurred. How do you dock his pay for insubordination or put her on probation for constantly showing up late without destroying the family equilibrium and incurring the wrath of the people you have to spend Thanksgiving with? When a boutique owner I know fired his sister for hiding serious accounting errors, their mother stopped talking to him for six months as punishment. Your childhood home and its inhabitants are always next door to the office when you and your siblings work together.

�֍

Ted Murphy knew better than to hire his unstable younger brother, Ryan, for a regular salaried position in his thriving fitness business, but he made a big mistake when he thought that he could put Ryan in charge of a construction project with impunity. Every conflict the brothers had as children resurfaced, and new ones from their adult lives were added to the mix, making this seemingly charitable move a nightmare for both of them.

Ted, a fitness guru who is now sixty and the eldest of six, has come a long way since he worked as a high school gym teacher in his twenties. By age forty his innovative Eastern-inspired training techniques had made his name in the industry, and he has since built an exclusive niche business with worldwide franchises and a clientele that includes celebrities and heads of state. Always the most responsible and now also the most successful of his siblings, he strives to create jobs for them at his studios, often overlooking or failing to anticipate problems that should be obvious. These efforts have backfired more than once and have caused more rancor than gratitude, but he persists for reasons that have to do with the past.

Ryan's life followed the opposite trajectory from his brother's. Ted and Ryan, who is two years younger, shared a room as boys, which was a trial for Ted both because of the way Ryan behaved and how their parents, who favored their second son, indulged him. "He had terrible tantrums, while I was the well-behaved, dependable, do-the-right-thing one," Ted recalled, without obvious rancor at this unfair treatment.

Even when Ryan was diagnosed with a behavior disorder, their parents still idealized him. "I never showed the talent that he did, so I had to follow the rules, but he got away with everything. My grades had to be good, and his were just ok, but he was this genius because of his high IQ score." Ted still accepts his parents' assessment of his brother's inherent superiority (even though it never came to fruition), but he clearly resents it.

Paradoxically, Ted owes his own innovative work to his father's attempts to control and denigrate him. "My involvement in sports was my way to create something of my own in an arena that didn't interest my father, where I could be free to have my own life," he said. Despite the family's preconceived notions, he proved to be extremely gifted in his chosen field. Meanwhile, his brother fell apart; Ryan "never went to college, took vast quantities of drugs, and was an alcoholic until age thirty-five. Then he cleaned up his act for a while, until he started abusing prescription drugs," Ted reported. He also described Ryan as "a control freak with an unhealthy relationship with money," qualities that had made him virtually unemployable (his wife supported him) and certainly did not bode well for any future collaboration. In contrast, Ted, the teetotaler and exercise aficionado, told me "I've always known what I wanted to do." As an adult, Ryan tried to copy Ted, moving to the same town and building a house there right after his brother did. The complete role reversal of the brothers in the present, I thought, must be a secret source of distress, guilt, gratification, and triumph for the non-"genius."

Ted has helped Ryan financially numerous times over the years, none of which has made any lasting difference. Although Ted acknowledges that filial loyalty is strictly a one-way street ("You can't ask Ryan to do anything. I'd call friends before I'd call him—he lets me know it's not convenient") and that Ryan never shows gratitude ("Whenever I give him work, he becomes resentful"), he cannot refuse. "I make money while I'm sleeping," Ted explained. "Ninety-nine percent of the time I'll say yes. I feel privileged and grateful to be able to help when I get a chance." He thinks of his beneficence as a far simpler action than it is.

Last year Ryan called and told his brother that his house was going to be foreclosed in fourteen days. "He never explicitly asked for help, just announced he was going to lose it," Ted said. "I couldn't risk giving him a job directly, so I had his wife do a project for me because she's reliable. But he was graceless about the whole thing; he said he could feel my disapproval even though I was careful not to be overbearing. It's hard for him to take work from my success when he's failing." Ted's simplistic explanation of why he continues to bail out a brother he does not respect or trust is "I'm not good at remembering problems," when in fact he is a master at denying them.

When Ted and I spoke, he had just hired Ryan once again—this time as an independent contractor to head a major construction project at his headquarters. "I couldn't give him work from my business that he couldn't do—that wouldn't be fair to my employees," he said, somehow having convinced himself that this circumscribed assignment would be different.

It was Ryan's second week, and Ted was full of hope. "If it could only be this good all the time—he's enjoying doing the renovations for us and doing them well. He even brought me some soup and some music today. I'm helpless in the things he's doing for me, and I let him know." The eternal optimist tried to shore up his brother's self-esteem without seeing that his words of praise would be interpreted as condescending. How long would this harmony last?

Six months later I learned that the job, which was supposed to have been finished in three months, was completely stalled, at enormous cost in revenue and staff morale. A year later the space was finally functional, though still unfinished, because Ted had turned the work over to his competent and reliable son-in-law, who only accepted the assignment on the condition that Ryan be banished from the construction site. I was not sanguine that this saga would not be repeated ad infinitum.

Even if, unlike Ted or Ryan, a working sibling longs to update her position in the family hierarchy, she may find breaking free from old patterns of relating next to impossible. For seventeen years, forty-one-year-old writer and copy editor Diana Montgomery has been sitting on the board of directors of the discount department store corporation started by her parents and their own contentious siblings. The forty-nine-year-old CEO, her older brother, Ethan, should by rights be answering to her, but instead secretly envies her and treats her as his inferior, just as he did when they were children. Only her earnings as a shareholder prevent her from quitting.

"He's extremely controlling, both in the decisions he makes and the insulting way he treats me," Diana said tremulously, clearly troubled by her predicament and chafing under her brother's yoke. "It took me sixteen years of working with him to figure out what I wanted and to stop reacting to him just because he was my brother. I haven't liked him or trusted him personally for a long time, although I still did financially, but even that's gone now."

Instead of turning to his board for advice and consent, as the head of a company is supposed to do, Ethan acts first and informs Diana—who is often the lone dissenter—later. "A year ago he took me aside and said, 'I want these two men to be co-CEOs, and I've already told them. I'm going to be out of here by age fifty-five,'" she told me. Not only was his decision presumptuous, but it had disastrous consequences, since one of the unilaterally chosen successors turned out to be a thief.

Diana dealt with her outrage and insecurity by withdrawing. "I've absented myself more and more," she said. "We barely talk now; I'm extremely guarded around him. He always needs to undercut me—at the last board meeting he mentioned apropos of nothing that I had gotten fired from my job. Things like that make me lose my equilibrium—why should I be the one who gets hurt?" I wondered what in their history made him perpetrate and her tolerate such humiliating treatment.

Ethan's behavior as a CEO mirrors his behavior as a brother and as a least favored sibling whose position shifted radically when his parents turned to their only son to run their company. As a child he expressed his jealousy of Diana, the baby their father doted on, by tearing apart her doll. "He was an awful big brother," Diana said. There was a decade-long rapprochement between them when she became a teen-ager, but it was entirely on his terms. "He was my mentor, and I was his little pupil. It was the first time in my life he paid attention to me," Diana recalled, with more bitterness than tenderness. "He was an English teacher, and he taught me how to think and read and study. But once I didn't want mentoring there really was nothing good left. He treats my older sister more like a peer now, but he never made that switch with me; I'm still the little sister." Despite their transitory period of closeness, Ethan could never consider Diana his equal; childhood rivalry resurfaced as soon as she stopped be-ing his acolyte, and she became a threat and a target once more.

A tumultuous relationship with his parents complicated Ethan's eventual position as heir to their company and con-tributed to his authoritarian stance with his younger sister. "I always thought taking over the business was his choice, but a year ago he told me that our father had called him in the mid-dle of the night and said, 'It's yours now,'" Diana reported. Even though Ethan had a doctorate in American studies and wanted to be a writer—as his sister eventually became—he needed a job, so he reluctantly accepted an offer that was more like an order, as his impulsive arrangements for an early exit make clear. He must have resented that the only duties of the baby of the family were to attend board meetings, express her opinions, and collect dividends, while he, the eldest, was held accountable by his punitive father for the bottom line. Being the one in charge of a family business does not insulate the chairman of the board from rivalry, envy, or anxiety. Diana's resentment, however, blinded her to her brother's dynamics and kept her locked into her role.

Ethan's position in the family had always been problematic. Long before the business was foisted on him, he had fled the country and remained incommunicado for two years, which made his parents, for whom appearances were everything, anxious and ashamed because they considered his departure a terrible reflection on them. "He told them he'd never speak to them again because they disapproved of his girlfriend," Diana recalled. "They didn't know where he was all that time, and they made up stories and pretended to friends that they did, although everybody knew the truth." To ensure their son's fidelity in the future, they tiptoed around him forevermore, taking his side and backing his management decisions even when he was wrong; as often happens, parental anxieties trumped their business judgment. They fail to protect Diana from him now just as they failed to punish Ethan for destroying her precious possession as a child or to understand the meaning of his aggressive act.

Despite his parents' belated support, Ethan still feels rejected and unfulfilled; tearing Diana apart emotionally gives him a sense of power. As in many family enterprises, the founders' involvement with the company they created did not stop when the children took over, but continues in insidious ways, and parallels their missteps as parents. This is one reason why legacy businesses often implode after two generations; research has shown that 25 percent of family businesses survive to the second generation and only 13 percent make it to the third.

Unresolved struggles between the elder Montgomerys and their own siblings continue to resonate, providing a template for the conflicts between their children. "My mother has two brothers who don't speak," Diana said, "and we have completely replicated my father's relationship with his sister as well—he hates her, and yet they have dinner every single Friday night of their lives." Unfortunately, knowing that they are reproducing a destructive pattern of dissimulation, underground hostility, and distrust does not motivate the heirs to change it. "I was told all my life that my aunt was silly and frivolous, and now I'm in the same position as she was," Diana noted. "We were all aware of the dysfunctional relationships our parents had with their siblings, but we didn't see it happening to us until it was a total replay." Why do they both passively accept the status quo?

Diana behaves as if altering their dynamics is entirely out of her hands, as it was when they were both children. "We were put in that role, and we keep acting in that role. We've said we don't want to be here, and yet here we are. In theory I hate my position, but in reality I can't get past the way he acts and how I react. I try, but I ask myself, how can I change it?" For example, she complained that Ethan had invited friends of his to a private family dinner without consulting her. "What could I do?" she asked—never considering that she could have told her brother that she did not appreciate his conduct and that he was not to repeat it if they were to continue having dinner together. This would be a notable departure from the way their father and aunt conducted themselves and could set the stage for other changes. Even if Ethan stayed the same, she would feel less at his mercy if she took charge.

Holding grudges is the weapon the whole family relies upon. Diana believes that staying mad is her only source of power over her manipulative brother, even if it forecloses any real communication between them. "I'm not giving an inch. My brother says he wants to sit down and talk, and I've refused every time. I want to stay angry because I can't trust him. I don't want to be talked out of that; he's very good at disarming people." Since she is convinced that Ethan is stronger than she is, she thinks that telling him frankly how untrustworthy she finds him would be dangerous rather than productive. On the other hand, Diana rightly fears that her anger rules her and prevents her from dealing with Ethan as an equal. "I feel so angry that I wouldn't have the kind of control I'd want if we were to discuss our conflict. I'd be an eight-year-old with a sixteen-year-old—he'd just laugh at me and drive off." She needs to investigate what keeps her from behaving in his presence like the self-aware forty-one year old she is, no matter how childish she may feel; if he tries to "drive off" now, she has the wherewithal to pursue him.

Diana is often lobbied by family members to patch it up with Ethan, but she has no illusions. "My parents think I should try harder. He keeps complaining to my mother and aunt, and they assure me that he really wants to change, but I tell them that until he actually acts differently, he's still an asshole." Yet since she never tells him directly how she feels, the spell cannot be broken, so she remains in her fantasy a sulking child cowering before a sneering bully of a teenage brother. Mutual suspicion and old resentments keep these siblings from approaching each other forthrightly, or from making the effort to understand each other's vulnerabilities and fears so that they could conduct themselves differently than their parents did.

Barring an unlikely change of heart in either sibling, the only thing that could break this stalemate is the death of their parents. Without their interference, Ethan and Diana might learn to separate family dynamics from corporate affairs. "After our parents are gone, Ethan and I probably won't get together for the holidays; it's sad," Diana said, with surprising regret that may indicate latent positive feelings about her brother. "My five-year-old daughter adores him. There may be a little more space when we're not intertwined the way we are now." Less fear, more frankness, and a little mutual recognition can help colleague/siblings like these stop repeating history.

✤

Bernie Wexler did not have the option about whether or not
to participate in his family's business: His older brother stole
it, with their parents' compliance, and forced him out. Only a
terrible twist of fate partially righted this wrong.

Bernie, now a sixty-six-year-old classics professor, is the
middle of three sons of a self-made entrepreneur who spent
fifty years creating a multimillion-dollar real estate empire in
the Chicago area. Bernie's brother Dan, two years younger
than he, became a dentist and moved away. He stayed unin-
volved in the company, while Bernie, who resembled his father
in temperament and business acumen, was recruited to over-
see daily operations and tenant relations in the buildings they
owned. He performed this job with expertise and relish—
until Ira, the firstborn son, a lawyer like their father and two
years older than Bernie, joined the firm a few years later, when
they were still both in their twenties. Unbeknownst to Bernie,
Ira immediately began insinuating himself with their father,
undermining his brother behind his back while working side
by side with him.

"He always had the ability to think exclusively about himself," Bernie told me. "We didn't talk much as children, and
we never had the closeness and trust on a deep level that Dan
and I did. Ira had a veneer of friendliness, but he was sorely
lacking in loyalty and personal integrity, and it was not entirely his fault; there was so much pathology in the family. He

was desperate to get something, to make his mark on the world." So desperate was he that he sacrificed his brother to his ambition without a moment's hesitation.

Bernie, steadfast and loyal, never suspected that Ira, while keeping up a façade of brotherly camaraderie ("He was always pleasant in the office—he even suggested that we buy property together") was scheming to discredit him in their father's eyes so that he could eventually divert Bernie's share of the inheritance into his own pocket. A problem with a tenant gave Ira the opening he needed to sow suspicion. "Ira got into a fight with somebody living in one of our buildings and told our father that I was responsible, although I had nothing to do with it. He never blamed me directly—it was all by innuendo—but he made our father fear a lawsuit." For the next several years, Ira built on this foundation until he achieved his goal. With their father's acquiescence, he won the competition to be the chosen one that Bernie never even knew was taking place.

Bernie learned the truth by degrees. "Ira was managing the building I lived in with my wife and family. When I wanted to rent an office that became available there, he refused to give me a break on the rent. He quickly rented it out to another tenant without telling me, because I would have found out when the lease was signed that he owned this huge, wealthy building worth eight million dollars. He had cajoled my father into giving it to him, and my father had gone along with it. My parents didn't tell me that my home belonged to my brother;

the tenant did." This was outrageous enough, but it was only the beginning.

How did the Wexler brothers' father permit one son to poison his relationship with the other? The stage was set when they were children. During those troubled years, Dan kept to himself and Ira allied himself with his father, while Bernie was the only one who took his father on. He alone objected to Mr. Wexler's arbitrary rules, his rages, his miserliness, and his need to control the entire household; their mother never intervened. Mr. Wexler felt a kinship with his middle son but also saw him as a rival, feeling threatened by Bernie's independence of mind and refusal to be silenced. "Ira knew not to stand up to him and never challenged him, so he got more attention from my father, but I always stood up to him, and he didn't like that," Bernie observed. The more compliant and devious Ira was the favored firstborn, Dan was the baby, and Bernie's position in the household was that of adversary and black sheep. These roles continued, as they usually do, when their father became the two elder brothers' employer. "I'd worked for my father as long as Ira did, and I had more responsibility, but he never valued my work and always paid him more, ostensibly because he was a lawyer," Bernie said. "You can live in the same family and be treated so differently, like you live in different worlds."

Bernie had to leave the firm after he discovered how his father and brother had treated him—the building turned out to be only one of many secret "gifts" worth many millions that

Ira obtained—so he went to graduate school, studied the classics, and essentially separated himself from his family. For the next several years he barely spoke to any of them but Dan, and he struggled to create an independent life far different from the one that was rightfully his. But even then he did not know the full extent of his father's rejection and his brother's betrayal. The way he found out, and what he found out, was as tragic as it was shocking.

Ira seamlessly took Bernie's place in the business and enjoyed his position, with its financial perks, offering no apology and attempting no rapprochement with the brother he had ousted. Then, when Ira was thirty-five, disaster struck. After suffering a seizure at the office, he was diagnosed with an aggressive brain cancer the size of a grapefruit and was given a year to live.

Bernie, struggling to put his feelings aside, went to visit Ira. He found his brother in a pitiable state but as manipulative as ever, even from his hospital bed. Their conversation and its aftermath revealed the full extent of Ira's treachery:

> As soon as he saw me, he turned to me and said, "Look out for my wife. Promise me that you won't let our father take away from her what she has; I know you're a rock." I gave him my word. It turned out that what she had was a vast amount of our family property and the right to half the estate, including my share—he had arranged for me to get both robbed and disinherited. This odd subterranean event was hidden by my

brother; he was as much a coward about confronting me as he
had been about confronting my father when we were children. When I found out the truth, I refused to talk to him,
even though he had a death sentence. I looked at him as a
scumbag. He knew he could rely on me, but I couldn't rely
on him. He wanted me to sacrifice my interests, to sacrifice
my life, to protect his wife—not even himself. I knew that
someone who dealt with his own brother in such a shame-
less manner was a weasel, that he'd bite the person helping
him on the neck where he couldn't see it. I saw how cold
he was.

The reactions of his father and brother when Bernie confronted them were devastating but entirely predictable. "My
father was a wall of ice when I tried to talk to him about it,
and my mother stayed out of it entirely," Bernie recalled. "Ira
said, 'Even though I have brain cancer, I'm not depressed like
you.' He had no understanding of integrity and could only
think about ways to raise himself up." Closeness to the grave
had not improved Ira's character; even then he had to an-
nounce his superiority over the childhood rival he still envied
even after stripping him of his rights.

At that point Bernie had no more illusions about family
solidarity or even decency, but nevertheless it grieved him that
his brother was dying so horribly, and he decided to visit him
once more as his condition worsened. Ira didn't disappoint
the last time they saw each other. "I went to the luxurious es-

tate he'd been given and that I knew he enjoyed," Bernie reported, "and he asked me, 'Why can't you let it go?' I said, 'It was an unforgivable thing,' and he said, 'I'm dying,' so I said ok, that I would spend time with him, and I was friendly to him again because I keep my word." When I asked Bernie why he did not reject Ira when he finally had the chance, he said, "I sure as hell didn't want to behave like him—I found him revolting." Bernie reconciled, at least superficially, with his brother to affirm his own sense of values and prevent himself from being contaminated by revenge, so he treated Ira with gentleness while judging him internally—a profound and humane solution.

Bernie told me the story of their last afternoon together. "Ira was in a wheelchair. He said he wanted to go around and look at the property, so I said I would take him. But the ground was uneven, and he was scared. 'Will I be ok?' he asked me. 'Sure,' I said. 'Nothing can happen. These wheels are big and easy for me to control—I can pick this whole thing up if necessary.'" Bernie both reassured (and literally supported) his helpless brother while asserting strength that was moral as well as physical. "I took him to every segment of his property—to see the canal he'd dug, the plantings he'd made, the ducks he'd raised. He thanked me—and he was sincere."

Bernie's empathy and compassion for Ira continued to the end. "After that he was unconscious, but I spoke to him anyway. I spent time at his bedside in case he was able to feel in that state, in case what he was feeling was that he was alone in the world and he didn't want to be." He refused to abandon the man who had abandoned him.

Ira's death brought their father to his senses, and he reconciled with Bernie, reinstating both his inheritance (minus the gifts that Bernie had inadvertently helped Ira's wife retain) and his place in the family, which was far more important to Bernie. At the eleventh hour, this highly critical man was even capable of taking pride in his son's achievements and told him so, offering at last the acknowledgment Bernie had always longed for; the prodigal father returned and was forgiven by his son, who had never stopped loving or admiring him. Bernie took devoted care of Mr. Wexler when he, too, became ill, and they were able to have several years of genuine intimacy before he died. Even though the family business was no longer there for Bernie to run and he keenly felt the loss, he found satisfaction in another profession.

⚜

Thirty years have passed since Ira's death. I asked Bernie whether his attitude toward Ira and what had happened between them had changed. "Just a little," he said:

> I recognize that as I think about him over the years, I think more and more about his weakness. It was disturbing to me that he was like that. I don't have much of a relationship with him in my own mind now—he was my brother without really

being my brother, more a brother in name than in fact. I have friends who are brothers; Ira wasn't. I see him as a grasping man and successful only at that. He doesn't share in the spirit of the life that I've lived. He couldn't comprehend anything about the way I operate and had no concern for my well-being. He was a sneak—that's the way he did things—he kept things hidden while he was stealing from me behind my back; he gave away his soul. I don't forgive him; I don't blame him or have anything against him—I'm more neutral. He kind of canceled himself out, and this is what's left.

Despite his opinion of Ira, Bernie kept his word to him and has continued to invite Ira's wife, who has long since remarried and retained a disproportionate amount of what should have been his own fortune, to all family affairs.

Bernie lost his position of power in his father's empire, a great deal of money, and his biological brother. But what he gained mattered more. He asserted his character and his integrity and became the undisputed boss of the most important business of all: his own life.

CHAPTER 6

FIVE VARIETIES
OF SIBLING STRIFE

⁜

When I tell someone that I'm writing about sibling strife, I'm surprised how often I get the same reaction: a sharp intake of breath, a look or nod of recognition, and then a flood of words—some descriptive, some defensive—about a relationship gone bad or one that was never very good in the first place. I went to my doctor's office recently, and her nurse, whom I have known casually for years, asked me what I was working on. I told her and saw her usual breezily friendly manner harden. She said, "My sister came out angry. She was always furious and sometimes even violent. I used to make allowances because she's my sister, but you get to a certain age and you don't want to take it any more." Then I saw the doctor, who also asked me about my project, and I got another earful from this usually reserved woman. "I found a lump in my sister's breast that turned out to be cancer," she said, with a bitter edge in her voice that I had never heard before. "Several months later she told me that she'd seen a doctor who gave her the best breast exam she'd ever had. You'd think she'd think that the one I gave her, which actually saved her life, was really the best." The tone of both these women was distressed, perplexed, and disappointed, and I got the feeling, as I usually do, that there was much more under the surface that rarely gets discussed with anybody—and certainly never directly with the person who provokes the feelings.

Unfriendly siblings never cease to be a thorn in our sides. They violate deeply held notions of what this relationship is supposed to be like, that even if you are not soulmates, you are not enemies or strangers. At very least, brothers and sisters should to be loyal and reliable, well disposed and concerned about your welfare. Whether unfriendly siblings are bums or investment bankers, our reactions to them are surprisingly similar: nagging distress when the subject comes up; some level of self-blame for the tension or trouble between you; the need to justify, with compelling examples, why there is bad blood or limited contact. I have never seen anybody describe one of these relationships with equanimity because family is what we have been taught to count on, and in adulthood siblings, however unsatisfying, are often the only family we have left.

A bad sibling is different from a bad parent. By midlife, most people have given up trying to change their aging parents and make efforts to come to terms with them because they realize the significance (and the time limits) of the relationship. But a sibling is a peer and somehow expendable. That bond feels less central to your own destiny or emotional health. There is much less urgency about addressing problems that you imagine you can simply avoid. But siblings are as much a part of our present as our parents, and perhaps even more important for our future. The more troubled the relationship, the more power it has over us.

There are five basic categories of problem siblings, with many permutations and combinations: the hostile and the envious, as represented by the sisters of my doctor and her nurse, the perpetual stranger, the chosen one, and the underachiever. Each type causes sorrow, frustration, helplessness, and a sense of being cheated out of one of life's fundamental comforts. The travails of several of the sibling couples that follow are probably set forever, but others hold surprising intimations for the future, turns of fate and opportunities for change they never would have imagined possible.

I. Grabbing a Knife by the Blade: Hostile Siblings

"THE FRIEND OF FLIPPER"
Passionately held convictions—particularly with a nonviolent veneer—provide a perfect stick to beat one's siblings with. Since she joined PETA seven years ago, Tom Keegan's older sister Maggie has been driving her entire family crazy, never missing an opportunity to torment them with her relentless

animal advocacy. Ironically, expounding a militantly non-violent philosophy allows her to express with complete self-righteousness the hostility she has harbored all her life. "She's always been difficult, but PETA has made her unbearable to the entire family," her brother told me, with a mixture of annoyance and sadness. "Prior to her conversion, we could cope, we could put some of it on hold, but now we can't see her without getting a lecture on cruelty to animals, why we shouldn't eat meat—she's very dramatic."

It is the use Maggie makes of her principles that infuriates Tom, not that they differ from his. "Maggie's twin sister is very far to the left, and I'm a right-winger, but we get along fine because she maintains civility—she doesn't confront," he explained. "But Maggie's a domineering, entitled person; a seam of bitterness runs through her. PETA encourages people to speak out, and I think she was waiting her whole life for somebody to give her the green light. Now that she's a Friend of Flipper, she assumes you're part of the problem. She took my thirty-five-year-old daughter to lunch and told her that she couldn't order a chicken sandwich. When my daughter said she'd pay for her own lunch, Maggie said, 'You're with me and this is what you'll have.'"

Tom's breaking point came when Maggie made a scene at his daughter's wedding. "On this very joyous day, my sister goes up to the in-laws and asks what they did with their cats when they came to town for the wedding. They said they had left them overnight at home with food and water, and she said, 'Real cat people would never do this.' I wanted to strangle her—where are your manners? My sister has found the ultimate dependent group to use against us; her screen saver is a circus elephant with a chain on its leg. This is a religion, and the price of admission is that you have to be as judgmental and crazy as she is."

Religious extremism runs in the family. "I've always felt Maggie was like my mother, who was a fanatical Catholic," he said. "You could never argue with her; there was nowhere to go with it. That was her way to deal with a disappointing life." Although the seven children in the Keegan family had "an early life of turbulence," with alcoholism and terrible marital discord, the other six "got out of most of it" and went on to have good relationships with one another. Tom, the youngest child by many years, was able to distance himself ("It was like watching a drama unfold," he observed), but clearly Maggie got caught in the middle and has finally found a way to express her long-held anger and frustration by berating them all. She has even managed to alienate her own twin; "They are done," Tom said.

When I asked Tom if there was anything that he missed about his sister, his tone became surprisingly wistful. "I would have abandoned her a long time ago if she wasn't also fun and sarcastic. I'd love to hear her tell me she's never seen anyone as gorgeous as my grandkids. My sister's good at this— she can be charming. I've been loyal, and kept my patience, because there's so much wreckage in my family. We could still spend time together—it would be great—but you can't with PETA."

I wondered if he could imagine Maggie changing. "Sometimes zealots get sick of being zealots," he said, "but I think it's over. The sad thing is that it's a loss now that our kids are having kids. She could certainly be civil three or four times a year. I miss Christmas, but the price is just too high. She's so brittle—she'll explode or fall apart if you say anything. I would wonder what I was doing there. She weighs one hundred pounds and I weigh two forty; I could probably crucify her if I wanted to." As he well knows, hostility begets hostility, but he controls himself even if she does not. "I'm just sick of looking the other way," he said, in a tone that was both defeated and fed up. "It's easier not to be there. This is an abyss; it has no bottom—you just have to avoid it."

"ICY STARES AND CUTTING GLANCES"

Tom finds his sister's browbeating infuriating, but Bonnie Shore actually fears her sister's violent deeds as well as her heated words, even though, like Tom, she detects the pain beneath the outrageous behavior. Bonnie, a fifty-eight-year-old medical technician, is grateful that her volcanic sixty-two-year-old sister, Kate, lives in another state, so that she only has to see her on family occasions. "Our relationship is very loaded," she said. "When we're together, all I get from her are icy stares and cutting glances. I don't share anything important. I very consciously don't make myself vulnerable to her because of the way she behaves. She frightens me—I don't know whether it's because something happened when we were children that I've blocked or just that she's pretty scary as an adult. Her rage has always been explosive and out of control."

Bonnie believes that anything she does can act as a trip wire for a punishing outburst. Kate's behavior at their mother's funeral five years ago confirmed Bonnie's worst fears. "Before we left for the service, she said she had a poem for us to recite at the graveside, and she asked me which verse I wanted to read. 'Any one you say,' I answered. She gritted her teeth and got fire in her eyes and screamed at her husband, 'I told you she wouldn't like the idea, that she doesn't want to do this! She never cares about me.' When we got to the cemetery, she stands by herself and glares at me throughout the ceremony. Afterwards she follows me to my car and starts banging on the car window. My father witnessed the whole thing. The next day my husband called their house, and her husband told him that she felt humiliated and had little memory of what had gone on. It was horrifying to me."

To Bonnie's relief, she was able to speak frankly to her father before his own death about her sister, and he acknowledged how difficult she had always been. Here is a case where a sibling's temperament and emotional disability are as much a source of discord as the way the parents deal with it; even concerted attempts to address a child's problems do not always work. "That was enormously validating for me," she recalled. But the repeated assaults she had endured made her unwilling to grant his dying wish. "He asked me to promise him to hold the family together after he died, but I don't see the benefit of holding something together when it's destructive," she said. Arm's length is the safest place to keep a sister like hers.

The severity of Kate's aggression makes Bonnie pessimistic about the odds of improving their relationship, especially since Kate is unwilling to investigate her own behavior and continues to blame Bonnie for the discord between them. "I suspect she can't self-soothe," Bonnie said. "Her rage is most intense when she's with me; when it's not expressed, I feel it anyway." But as Bonnie's insight into her sister has grown with the distance she has learned to keep from her, she sees something else that is just as troubling and just as unfixable: "When I look into her eyes I try not to make eye contact any more, because I see anger and rage as well as a deep dark sadness under the surface. I get pulled into this bottomless sadness like a vortex." Now she understands that dealing with the fury above as well as the despair below is a job for a therapist, not a sister.

"LIKE OIL AND WATER"

Sibling hostility, and its relatives bitterness and envy, can be expressed by furious outbursts, physical violence, or, as in the case of Deborah Anderson's younger sister, Ellen, hateful actions. Since the age of twelve, Ellen has been stealing from her sister and otherwise mistreating her, without remorse.

Deborah says that "Ellen has hated and rejected me all her life" because she had the drive to escape the strictures of their family while Ellen stayed put.

The Anderson sisters' home life was wretched. Their father was a traveling salesman who left them and their embittered, infantile mother at home for long periods; since she never learned to drive, they were often stranded without even the basics. "I was a different-world person; I always wanted more from life," Deborah told me passionately. Her sister, who was the mother's favorite and very much like her—Deborah was her father's daughter—had no such aspirations, but envied her elder sister's determination to better herself and punished her for it.

At fifteen Deborah got a job and began paying rent to her parents; later she became the only member of her family to attend college, eventually earning an advanced degree as well. In a perverse combination of identification and vengeance, Ellen stole the clothes that Deborah had bought with the money she proudly saved. The "borrowing" became ever more brazen. "She went on a hundred-mile trip with our stepsister and took my three best outfits and brand-new shoes," Deborah recalled. "When I objected, my mother said I was too hard on her, that she needed my things and I didn't. She always defended my sister's behavior and made it clear that I should be taking care of her." To make matters worse, Ellen's companions stranded her when they reached their destination, and her mother insisted that Deborah, who had just learned to drive, pick her up. "That was really hard on me," she told me matter-of-factly. "I had fifteen dollars to my name, and I had to drive all the way there by myself. I was scared to death. We didn't speak for a long time after that."

Ellen never apologized; "she thought it was ok to do that," Deborah recalled, still finding her sister's actions and her mother's attitude shocking forty years after the fact. "My sister never considered it a big deal to steal from me. I was furious and sad about it; it was harder on me than on her. Even then it was essential to me that people be ethical and honest. It hurts so much when a member of your own family does something like that." This episode and others like it drove Deborah to leave home a year later, never to return.

Leaving home was one more thing that Ellen could not forgive. "She hated me because I escaped," said Deborah, who eventually became an occupational therapist in a city on the other side of the state. "I got away, and she didn't want to. She's still working in a factory in the town where we grew up, although she makes much more than I do; you have to have something inside you that makes you want more out of life."

The personalities of the two sisters never meshed. "We fought all the time, from an early age. Ellen never felt comfortable around me; we've always had an estranged relationship, like oil and water," said the serious but soft-spoken elder sister. "She's always inventing reasons to be angry with me; at this point I couldn't get through an hour meeting with her. She has a mouth on her like a truck driver. There's a look about

people when they choose a certain life—hard, lots of ciga-
rettes, like they would bite your head off. She always blamed
my father for leaving her and blamed me because I was his
favorite. She's bitter and expresses it by being nasty to me."

When their mother died, Ellen stole from Deborah once
more. "She thought she had a right to look through everything of my mother's first before showing it to me, even the
photos; by the time I got there almost nothing was left."

Despite everything, Deborah has tried to connect with her
sister throughout the tragedies that befell both of them as
adults, but her efforts are never reciprocated. "She married a
guy who became an addict, and he was shot to death. I helped
her through all this, but when my own son was killed in a car
crash the next year, she put his picture away and never talked
about him again." Doing nothing to console her devastated
sister was the most hostile action of all.

II. The Sibling from Another Planet

"WE'D NEVER BE FRIENDS"/"I DON'T KNOW HIM"
Two friends of mine, Nina Pearson and Peter Siegal, have
brothers with whom they have absolutely nothing in common. Although both of them physically resemble their brothers, each of whom is two years younger, they inhabit different
psychic realities and do not speak the same emotional language. Nina seems more pained about this situation than Peter
does, as well as more sanguine about future possibilities for a

meaningful connection, but both of these introspective and attuned people feel that their brothers are closed doors and that they lack the password to get inside.

"Ed and I are family; we'd never be friends," says Peter, an aesthetic, cosmopolitan, sixty-year-old lab technician, of his brother, the Archie Bunkeresque truck driver. "We were just as estranged as kids as we are as adults—we weren't buddy brothers. I realized in my twenties that I didn't have a relationship with him and that I never had; it felt strange more than sad that he didn't exist very much for me."

Radical differences in temperament, worldview, and interests have made them strangers to each other all their lives. Peter, the older, academically minded son, was originally favored by both parents, while Ed was the troublemaker and the problem child, but this changed later on. "When we were younger, I was an extroverted intellectual," Peter recalls. "He was a D student, and I got As. Ed played hooky and got in trouble—he broke into people's houses with his friends. He was kept back in second grade and never went to college; in school the teachers said to him, 'You're nothing like your brother.'" The unspoken rivalry between the brothers continues in the present and contributes to their alienation from each other: "Ed lived in my shadow a lot. He's had to work his whole life to compete with me, but now he has the upper hand because he has the grandchildren. He's got a blue-collar job like our father, although he now makes a six-figure income."

His brother's unpredictable moods, authoritarian attitude, and prejudices—"Although he isn't even religious, Ed told his son, my favorite nephew, that my being gay is not right, and that God didn't approve of it"—make Peter wary of even the occasions when they seem to get along. "There are moments that it's all right to be with him and he acts like a mensch, but he can turn on a dime and lash out at me." Peter is grateful that Ed has been taking care of their mother and moved her into his house, but he sees no commonality with him beyond family obligation. "When she goes, any semblance of a relationship between us will probably go too," he assumes.

Had there ever been anything good between them? "We do share memories; it's the one thing that holds us together. My mother had pneumonia when we were kids, and we cried and held each other. I felt his support then, and I defended him sometimes—there were some tender moments. We didn't fight; we just lived parallel lives under the same roof. Recently my nephew asked me, 'Why are you and Dad not close? I get so much from being close to my brother,' and I said, 'We're from very different worlds. We're civil—we get along the way you do when you don't really get along. This is something that can't be fixed. It would take a huge amount of effort on both sides that neither of us is willing to make.'"

I asked Peter whether he had ever tried to talk to his brother about their relationship. "What's the use?" he replied. "I know he wouldn't understand. I don't think it's worth it; he doesn't have the insight to do that. Even if I explain something he doesn't get it. I don't feel there's much there. He's so rigid that it's hard to find things in common." Peter has tried to connect in basic ways, but Ed does not reciprocate. "Last year I cooked them a big dinner and they only stayed forty-five minutes. I never get invited to family weddings. Even the holidays are falling away now—he's going to his kids' houses for Christmas. It actually feels better; I wish it would have happened years ago."

Peter is fairly certain that history cannot be undone, but he still has some family feeling for the brother he could never talk to. "In the next stage of life, any contact between us would be based on whether one of us needs to help the other out in illness and aging, not because of our relationship." His feeling for Ed's sons is the one source of hope. "If Ed's still alive, resolution may come through them."

⚜

Nina Pearson showed me two photos of her brother, Michael—one of them from the 1970s in which he epitomized the "hip dude" of the period, in tight jeans, boots, and long hair, and a more recent one, in which his big, empty smile seems pasted on. Brother and sister looked alike—athletic and lively—in the earlier shot, but thirty years later I could not detect a resemblance. The contemporary image of Michael did not show a mean or bitter face, but its focus seemed entirely external, while she is one of the most deeply introspective people of my acquaintance.

"I don't know him," she said starkly. A relentless optimist, Nina yearns to know him in the future, and things that

Michael has said and done recently encourage her. But I got the impression that at the age of sixty he is still a cipher whose life remains largely unexamined and that she does most of the emotional work.

"Early on I felt very protective of him," said Nina. "We shared a bedroom, so we used to talk when privately tucked away, but it changed when I started junior high, and I have no idea what he felt towards me after that. That's when we started to have a divide. Both of us needed to escape a stressful environment—we saw my father hit my mother—but we went about it differently. He'd hang out at his basketball coach's house, and I got involved in the Girl Scouts. We never disliked each other; I admired him. He'd grasp things more quickly than I did, and socially he was much more at ease, such a cute guy and a sharp dresser. I was very surprised to learn from his wife in this past year that he was actually shy, and that he had a terrible temper, like our father, which I never saw either—we never fought."

Michael totally vanished from Nina's life when she left for college, and she had no idea why. "For some reason we didn't have a relationship after that; he didn't write to me. After he got married, he never called. I think he was declaring his own life." She excuses his neglect, blaming the roles they were assigned by their parents and his need to escape from their family. "I was the caretaker, and he was the hope, the son who was supposed to achieve," she explained. "He didn't feel the sense of responsibility that I did."

Nina went to remarkable lengths to try to maintain a bond with Michael, but he rebuffed her efforts, even after she took the extreme step of apologizing to him in case she had unintentionally offended him. "When I hadn't heard from him for about five years, I finally decided to write a letter saying that if I'd done anything, I was sorry and that he should tell me—it was very, very difficult for me not to know what the hell was going on. I heard nothing; he just didn't get it. This made it clear that he didn't want to work on the relationship, that he wasn't going to put in the effort. It was brutal."

Despite behavior that would cause most people to stop trying—he seated her far away from his family when she made the trip to attend his daughter's wedding, took no share in caring for their dying mother, and cheated her out of part of her inheritance—Nina's sense of loyalty and her desire to maintain a family tie are unshakable. Michael's shutdown state makes her feel compassionate, not cold. She forgives everything, insisting that there is still something worth pursuing.

It is possible that she is right because there have been some encouraging signs lately. "He's gotten divorced and has a new woman in his life. He invited me to stay with them for a few days, and it felt like we were friends, like none of this existed. If he'd been cold or nasty, it would have been different, but I could tell there was a person there. And he said some interesting things—that he wished he had traveled the world as I had, that I was more independent than he was. I was shocked because I always thought that he was the freer of the two of us.

We still look very similar; we could almost be twins—people think we are. We're so alike; our cores are alike. Some of his ways are quite different; that's what separated us. I think being a sibling represents that painful history, and he's done no work on understanding himself, while I try so hard to transform myself. He doesn't even know what he should be dealing with. Now at least I can tell from what he says that he's thinking about our relationship."

How far that thinking goes remains to be seen.

She had a touching dream after her visit that reflects her vision of recovering their original bond, which she thinks of as a certainty when it may be no more than a loving hope: "I saw my brother and me with white hair. We were much older, and we were good friends. I knew from that image that we'd be close again one day, and I realized that now he may be in transition and that moving in a new direction in his life will allow him to have much more insight. I absolutely expect it, if nothing else because I'm his sister. What a gift to be able to help him do it if I can!" If anything can motivate a man to consider his life, having a sister like this would make it worth doing.

III. The Favored Sibling

"HE HAD IT; I DIDN'T HAVE IT"

"I see Allen as perfect," says forty-three-year-old guidance counselor Heidi Forman of her brother, a "high-level businessman" who is two years older and a dazzling success at everything he touches. She speaks with conviction, without the slightest doubt that her assessment is the objective truth. "He's also personable, engaging, and genuinely nice—not a jerk," she explains, at once appreciative and envious. Allen was a tough act to follow. "And he's always been the favorite. From the time I was a baby, I could tell my mother adored him. He was her love, the shining star. The response I elicit is different: He had it; I didn't have it. I've always wondered, 'How does he do it?'"

Even now, as a professional and a woman about to give birth to her second child ("Sibling issues are really salient for me now," she said), she inevitably comes up lacking in comparison. Despite her recognition of family dynamics, Allen's superiority seems both intrinsic and immutable, rather than created and maintained by their mother's undisguised preference. The contrast between them is excruciating. "It's an incredibly painful situation," Heidi candidly admits. "At the core I feel there's something wrong with me. I'm so vulnerable—I don't want to advertise this."

Heidi told me that she has taken the rare step of actually speaking to Allen about their relative ranks in their mother's affections. "I said, 'I think you were favored,' and he agreed. When I asked him how it affected his life, he said, 'I feel completely confident that all will go well, that I'll get a positive response.'" I noticed that Allen did not pursue the conversation his sister initiated, never asking how their mother's flagrant preference for him affected her. This is almost always an uncomfortable topic for those on top; guilt and unconscious awareness that one's position is unfair cause the preferred child not to inquire too closely into this happy arrangement.

A surprising and troubling wrinkle emerged as we explored Heidi's relationship with her brother: Despite protestations of inferiority and struggles with insecurity, she has actually spent much of her life concealing superior abilities, talents that most people (and most parents) would be proud of. "I always did better than my older brother in school," she said, almost as an afterthought. "I skipped a grade, and he was held back. We went to the same school, and nobody knew we were siblings." Competition was far more mutual, and Allen's rise to the top was actually slower and more problematic than it appeared to her. "I learned that his son was held back too. Allen didn't tell me this, and he never told his son that the same thing had happened to him," Heidi revealed. "I was also a more talented musician than Allen; when he took piano lessons, I taught myself how to read music on my own and learned what he played. I wanted to study piano myself, but my mother said no because she was afraid I would overshadow him." Their mother not only favored her son; she actively sabotaged her daughter's success.

As is so often the case, Mrs. Forman reproduced with her children the pathological sibling hierarchy in her own family. "My mother's mother adored men," Heidi told me. "My mother had a brother who was also accomplished and successful—he was groomed for that. My mother became a doctor, but she worked for three dollars and fifteen cents an hour in a socialist health clinic. I got the message I shouldn't earn lots of money, that there was something vulgar about having that as a focus. As a result, I don't compete; I retreat. I've always stayed on the lowest rung of the ladder; I got a master's degree instead of a Ph.D."

Heidi's mother kept her daughter in the same inferior position in which she had been placed by her own mother, and, until now, Heidi complied because she wanted to keep whatever fragment of her mother's love that she could by staying in the place assigned to her—another typical scenario. Allen was their mother's masculine self; Heidi, the repudiated feminine one. "I've always thought of myself as a loser. I've never been comfortable winning. I've held myself back and let somebody else go ahead. What else could I do to be loved?" she asked, regretfully.

But things may be changing. Heidi is beginning to challenge her assumptions about her place in the world. "Allen's not afraid to win," she observed. "I've watched him establish constant dominance all these years; I never dared to compete with him because I assumed until now that it was impossible to succeed." She never realized before that her brother had been anxiously aware of her abilities, that he had concealed (but not escaped) intense shame and had covertly competed with her. Blinded by her own envy and sense of inferiority, she failed to recognize his. Now she is starting to recover memories that show a far less seamlessly confident side of her brother. "I remember that he teased me when he was picked on at school; he was small for his age. He only blossomed when he went away to school, and he never came back. Meanwhile, I got connected with a life that was not successful."

Although she claims to have "adored" Allen as a child and ceded all victories to him without a fight, things were not that simple. A dream she had at age seventeen showed her most deeply buried feelings: "When he was living overseas, I dreamed he died and that I was devastated. I woke up feeling the world was black." Unconsciously, she wanted to get rid of him for good, the only way to clear the way for herself.

Because Heidi has never let herself know about the dark side of their relationship, or recognized that potent childhood rivalry goes underground but does not disappear, she does not understand why their current bond is "superficial"; "I've just assumed this doesn't matter to him," she said. But now she sees that it must, whether her brother acknowledges it or not.

Heidi's own second pregnancy is affording her an unexpected opportunity to emerge from beneath her brother's shadow and to make a difference for the next generation. "I feel I may be shifting out of that idealization of him," she said excitedly. "I have discounted ways I was successful—I always thought that if I were to outshine him, my mother would crumble. This change has to do with the sibling on the way. Finding out that it's a boy and not a girl was a terrible disappointment at first—I was so identified with the girl who doesn't get as much as the older boy, so invested in compensating her. But now it's not going to be about who gets more attention or who's favored but about each child's becoming himself and recognizing each for who he is. I can do that!"

⨫

After our interview, I received a letter from Heidi describing the impact of her new insights about her relationship with her brother:

> One of most powerful things I understood as a result of our conversation was my brother's vulnerability. I have always viewed him as perfectly confident—perfect in every way. Our talk has just created a powerful internal shift from viewing myself as the flawed and vulnerable one to a more balanced view of us as two essentially human people. I haven't yet had a conversation with him about it, as he is overseas for the year, but I am planning to talk to him more about our dynamic as soon as he returns.

IV. The Green-Eyed Sibling

"WHEN I DO SOMETHING OF NOTE, IT'S VERY HARD FOR HIM"
Pam Ackerman's sixty-five-year-old brother, Ken, is thinking about retiring. This is strange because he has never held a regular job. "He's perennially unemployed—I'm endlessly self-employed," says the sixty-year-old dance teacher and arts

publicist, irony cloaking her profound disappointment and contempt for her brother's indolence. "His last job was part-time arts administration in the sixties, and he's complained about the lack of opportunities ever since. He should have been a musician, but instead he lives off money from my parents and his wife's salary while he constantly fights with her. I've been busy from the time I was born; my mother said I was never bored—I was doing, making up songs, dancing. Ken was extremely talented in music, writing, and painting, but he has made nothing of himself, so when I do something of note it's very hard for him."

The contrast between these two artistically gifted siblings, who used to perform at parties together when they were children, is dramatic. Pam has several careers in the arts and a lively marriage with a devoted husband who is also her business partner; she invested her share of the inheritance in their publicity firm. Ken dabbles in film but has little to show for it. The discrepancy in their adult lives is especially striking because, like Heidi Forman's brother, Ken had more freedom and encouragement as a child ("He was the son and the first-born, so he could do what he wanted, while I had to comply," Pam remembered). Meanwhile, Pam struggled with self-doubt and performance anxiety all her life but did not let either stop her. She has been slow to recognize Ken's discomfiture that he gave up while she prevailed.

The intensity and pervasiveness of her brother's jealousy are starting to dawn on her now. "We have a fine relationship in a way," she claimed. "He's a handsome, charming, bright guy with sex appeal; he looks good on the surface." But when she mimicked a typically passive-aggressive telephone message he'd recently left her—infuriatingly slow, depressed, withdrawn, and withholding—she had to admit laughingly that "he's a drag." Recently, Ken pressed Pam to advise him about a dispute he was having with his wife, but failed entirely to see that his own behavior had provoked it. "It was a big nothing," she said, unwittingly describing more than just this frustrating conversation.

Pam portrays Ken as a capable but secretly embittered and depressed man whose pride prevents him from working seriously at anything. He is mired in inaction, while she is a whirlwind of activity, passionately engaged with life. "I have watched my brother get stupid," she said sadly.

When she was younger, Pam's way of neutralizing Ken's envy without even letting it register was to try not to deserve it. "I didn't shine too much or draw attention to myself," she explained. "I was always ambivalent about being in spotlight even though I've always desired it. This internal habit made my dance career tormented and kept me from enjoying it as much as I should have." She has spent many years working through her struggles with self-expression.

Although relations between them are superficially cordial, Ken's negativity emerges subtly; there is a striking discrepancy in how they react to each other's ongoing creative endeavors. Pam has always been Ken's biggest fan, enthusiastically supporting anything he has a hand in from the front row, but he never reciprocates. Somehow the man without a job never has time to come to any of his sister's performances or productions. It hurts her that he cannot appreciate her success, especially after all the self-doubt she has had to overcome and the risks she has taken, and that he feels no brotherly delight in her achievement or pride in the effort she has put in over the years to make it happen. He cannot bear the comparison.

The most flagrant manifestation of a lifetime of covetousness occurred last year when Pam was offered a part in a theatrical production. She was thrilled and terrified about her upcoming performance. Of course, Ken failed to mention it in their regular phone conversations. This time, though, she decided to push him. "I didn't let him get away with avoiding it," she said. "I pointedly and repeatedly told him I really wanted him to come." Still, Ken did not tell her that he was attending until the last minute. He and his wife and son talked throughout the show, left abruptly, and never congratulated her. Even when she called him the next day and asked how he liked it, Ken could not be gracious; all he could offer his sister was a grudging "It wasn't my kind of thing."

Pam recalled something else that bothered her: When Ken saw that she was walking painfully because of an orthopedic injury, he never said a word. She was understandably upset that his self-involvement prevented him from showing the slightest interest or concern. Could he have been unconsciously pleased that she had finally been slowed down?

Like many relationships between siblings in conflict, theirs is complicated and not entirely devoid of warmth or devotion. "It's been friendly and supportive at times," Pam noted. "We've helped each other. He was a prince—better than me—at taking care of our parents when they were dying. And he was overjoyed at my wedding." Since he got married years before she did, I could not help speculating that it must have been easier for him to be unambivalently happy about seeing her at the altar than watching her on the stage.

Pam holds her brother responsible for his limitations, even as she recognizes the origins of his paralysis of will. "My father was very competitive with Ken; he was nicer to me. When I saw them interact, I really got how Ken was undermined, although he doesn't seem to realize it."

In the process of working through her own inhibitions, she has also accepted that she has a right to enjoy the life she has created. "I love Ken, and I feel bad for him, but I don't feel guilty," she said. "It's not my problem that he hasn't made a new friend in thirty-five years." Would she miss him if they never saw each other again? "I wouldn't because it isn't much fun to be with him, not much fun at all; he's a weight." The contrast between their lives and how Ken acts toward her because of it make a satisfying connection impossible. "For years it's been hard to have an interesting conversation—hard to have any real conversation, in fact. Anything I'm doing throws him, and he never acknowledges it. I think a lot about how the lives of the two of us with similar talents in the quartet of my family have had such strikingly different outcomes. After all, it's not like one wanted to lay bricks and the other wanted to write books. Everything's been lavished at his door. He's doing nothing with it."

V. The Incompetent Sibling

"I WENT TO HARVARD, SHE
DROPPED OUT OF COMMUNITY COLLEGE"
Michelle Marks has had so little contact with her younger sister, Marilyn, for so long that she doesn't know how old she is. The forty-year-old dermatologist is terribly embarrassed to admit it. "We just don't talk very much," she said, with a nervous laugh. "We have no communication with each other except when I go to visit my family. When we do it's friendly enough, but there's a big gulf between us; I've always felt very different from her."

On the surface, Michelle has everything and always did— brains, beauty, emotional and professional success, as well as a special place in her father's affections. "I was the outstanding sibling," she says straightforwardly, the kind of older sister that Marilyn, who was two years younger, and David, who was eight years younger, were encouraged to emulate and could not help envying for her obvious advantages. But her life has never been as unclouded as it seemed. "My parents divorced when I was six," she told me. "My father stayed in our house and we had to move out. From the third grade on I was the one who got the kids out the door to school in the morning because my mother went back to school. I did very well regardless, but they started falling behind."

Michelle tried desperately to compensate for her parents, both of whom abdicated their responsibilities and left her in charge. She remembers that her younger siblings "saw me as their parent. I felt I knew what they needed, and I tried to provide it," even at the expense of her own childhood. Her longing to be a child herself took the unusual form of asking to borrow her younger sister's clothes, which Marilyn staunchly refused to allow.

Michelle's father (and to a lesser extent, her mother) made her job even harder. His undisguised preference created an unbreachable barrier between her and Marilyn, who started having problems early on. "He was always comparing her to me, which set up a really horrible dynamic. My sister tried to do the same things I did, but she probably did them because my parents told her that 'Michelle did that.'"

Marilyn never got out from under the shadow of the star, which made the one resentful and the other terribly guilty. "She struggled to find what was important to her," Michelle recalled. "She was very afraid of lots of things when I wasn't—although she matured earlier than I did and had boyfriends before I did. Later on she got depressed and started drinking, and then she was caught stealing; the divide grew as we grew. There was an educational divide as well—I went to Harvard and she dropped out of community college." Marilyn found subversive ways to get back at Michelle, taking things as well as withholding things; "I invited her to visit me at college, and she slept with a friend of mine as an expression of her feelings toward me."

Reprising her stint as her sister's surrogate mother, Michelle tried to rescue Marilyn. "When I moved to Connecticut for medical school, she became seriously depressed, and I wanted her to come and live with me, which she did for a while. I've always felt that she's actually really smart, and I've encouraged her to go to therapy, but she refuses. She's afraid of confronting things." Michelle provided a temporary change of venue (and good advice that Marilyn probably considered condescending), but she could not change her sister's life unilaterally.

The trajectories of their destinies diverged ever more radically as Michelle fulfilled her early promise, married, and created a thriving medical practice, while Marilyn spiraled downward. With distress in her voice, Michelle detailed the difference in their lots, a difference that is not lost on Marilyn. "When my son started private school, she said, 'You think you're so fancy.' She recently left a secretarial job because of a conflict with her boss, so now she's a waitress at a diner. She smokes pot a lot. I know she's numbing herself."

So far, Michelle's story sounded like one I'd heard countless times before—one that in many ways I had lived myself with my own troubled brother. But the relationship between these two sisters has taken an entirely unexpected turn: Michelle has a serious illness that could kill her unless Marilyn donates a kidney to her. The life of the one who seems to have every-thing depends on the one who never got enough.

Michelle revealed her predicament in the most undramatic tone imaginable, doubtless to downplay the tragic irony of what she is facing. "I have a dilemma right now," she said. "I would like to be closer to her. To complicate my situation with my sister further, I have juvenile diabetes—I was diagnosed at eighteen—and I have kidney disease. My doctor has told me that some day I'll need a transplant. Poor Marilyn! She was going to give a stem cell transplant to save our brother, David, who had leukemia, but he died before it happened, five years ago." It horrifies Michelle to imagine that Marilyn might think that Michelle views her as the source of organs to be harvested for the benefit of others, that her only value is her physical assets.

When I asked Michelle how she plans to raise this excru-ciating subject with the sister whom she hardly sees, she said, to my surprise, "I've already asked her. I approached her and told her that I might possibly need a kidney transplant at some point." Anxiety made Michelle test the waters and present her condition as less dire than it really is to protect both her sister and herself from the fallout if Marilyn were to refuse.

"Part of me worries that Marilyn can't say no," she explained. "I'm afraid that she wouldn't tell me if she has any hesitation about doing this." The last thing Michelle wants is for Mari-lyn to think her sister feels entitled or to take her self-sacrifice for granted. "I don't want to treat her as if I expect it; that would make me seem even more arrogant and demanding than she already thinks I am." Michelle is worried that she has been too free with criticism and with unsolicited advice that must feel like criticism, and she fears that Marilyn believes, not without reason, that her sister disapproves of the way she lives. "I want her to do things, and she knows it. How many times have I told her, as if I know better, that 'You should finish college,' or 'Shouldn't you try to work it out with your boss?'" Michelle doesn't want to "jam things down her throat"—especially a demand like this.

The gap between their circumstances haunts the older sister. "I back off because I feel awful about her life. Taking a trip for her is a big deal—it's so hard to accept. And the saddest, most painful thing of all is that we're not close." All these things made Michelle hesitate to be completely frank with Marilyn about how grave her prognosis really is.

But she need not have been so careful. Marilyn understood immediately, and her response was straightforward and magnificent. "She said, 'I'd do that in a heartbeat,'" Michelle reported, weeping. "She was very, very generous. I just saw her, and I realized that she is so giving and loving."

But old habits die hard, even in extremis, and Michelle, as overcome with emotion as she was, was tongue-tied at first, unable to find the words to thank her sister. "I didn't say all that to her; I only told my friends. If it had been anyone else, I would have told her immediately how much it meant to me, but because it was her, I could only do it later. And when I said how moved I was and how much it meant to me, she said, 'I feel really fine about it. Organ donation brings a chain of love and good things.'" Michelle was overwhelmed and humbled to discover her sister's hidden depths.

I suggested that Marilyn might genuinely want to do something so meaningful, not only to be closer to her, but to make herself feel more powerful and to show that she is not just on the receiving end of her sister's advice and largesse. Michelle agreed, at least in principle. "It's a tremendous connection— it felt really great. I want to try to reach out to her and articulate that maybe this could bring us closer together." But there are lifelong barriers that an Oprah moment alone will not tear down. Michelle admitted, frankly, "We don't know how to be intimate with each other. We were always competing for resources, love, and attention. We were all on our own, and never got the opportunity growing up to be really close and connected. I feel like we both missed out, and it hangs over my head. But what she said, what she is offering me, eases my mind. I can actually feel myself relax. I want to tell her, 'You were perfect, and this is such a role reversal. I've felt the gulf between us all the time. I know our father poured lots of attention into me; he said 'You are our only hope.'"

"And now she's yours," I said. "Tell her everything."

Not even an organ transplant can magically erase years of dissension and alienation between siblings, but the spirit in which Marilyn is offering a part of herself, and Michelle is receiving it, gives each sister something precious from the other that they had no access to before.

CHAPTER 7

FOR THE SAKE
OF THE PARENTS

⁜

I. Aging Parents and Their Strife-Ridden Children

Dealing with aging, ailing, and dying parents and the problematic wills they often leave behind puts the final nail in the coffin of many a moribund sibling connection. The biggest crisis adult siblings face is managing the endgame and the joint decision-making it entails—no easy matter when you can barely have a civil conversation even under normal circumstances. The strain causes grievances and rivalries that have been buried since childhood to resurface with a vengeance: Who was the favorite? Who cares the most? Whose judgment prevails when there are differences of opinion? Where does the buck stop? Who does the dirty work? And who gets the china? Nevertheless, on rare occasions, undergoing these trials together actually breathes new life into a sibling relationship given up for dead.

Few people witness a parent's deterioration with equanimity; if they are mortal, so are we. Even where there is goodwill, everybody responds differently, some taking charge and others fleeing. But siblings who are already estranged and therefore wary of each other's motives find it nearly impossible to reach a consensus on how to handle the myriad emotional and practical crises that follow a serious diagnosis.

I know two brothers, David and Stan Singer, who were close in childhood and became increasingly alienated later in life. Their responses to their father's mental and physical ailments differed radically, reflecting both their disparate personalities and the unspoken tensions between them. The elder son, who was identified with and favored by the father, emphatically denied that anything was wrong with him, particularly cognitively, long after the damage was unmistakable; he was also doctorphobic, like his father. But the younger son, the deceased mother's favorite, was galvanized into action. Worried by his father's increasing confusion and mental lapses, as well as by his failing eyesight—he needed binoculars to watch television—this son arranged a neurological workup and felt grieved but not surprised when the diagnosis was dementia.

He immediately called his brother to discuss how to prevent their father from continuing to drive with these two dangerous disabilities. Outraged and anxious because the man who was his role model was declining precipitously, the elder brother appointed himself the defender of his father's independence, insisting that he was still "more than competent" to manage his own affairs and to make all decisions for himself, including staying behind the wheel if he wanted to; asserting that his father needed no care also conveniently excused him from providing any. The younger brother, worried and undaunted, hired a geriatric expert, who alerted the police in the town where the elderly man lived. As a result he was required to take a driving test and get an eye examination. When he failed both and his license was about to be revoked, the police discovered that it had in fact expired long ago and that he had not paid insurance premiums for years. They then confiscated his car keys.

"How could you embarrass him like this?" the furious elder brother said to the younger one. "You should thank me for saving his life, the lives of other motorists, and our inheritance," the younger brother responded. This was the first, and the last, frank exchange the brothers had during their father's final years. David provided tender, competent care to the end, and Stan did nothing at all but protest.

As their parents grow older most adults take a certain amount of role reversal for granted, accepting that they will now be giving care and their parents will be receiving it. Nonetheless, to the consternation of their self-reliant brothers and sisters, a surprising number of siblings revert instead to a second childhood themselves, turning to their elderly parents for financial assistance. Amy Kaplan's younger brother Ron went even a step further. At age forty he actually moved back into their seventy-five-year-old mother's house, the one in which he had grown up, and brought his wife and children along. So far they have stayed almost three years.

At a time when most mothers are slowing down, his mother is shopping, cooking, and cleaning up after him and his entire family. She supports her newly enlarged household with a part-time job (she had been living alone since her divorce decades earlier), while neither he nor his wife contributes towards their upkeep. Amy, fifty-three, is aghast and feels helpless to stop it.

Her daughter knows that Mrs. Kaplan is complicit in this perverse arrangement; she is not simply her son's victim. "My mother is upset, though she's not willing to take a stand," Amy told me. "She says, 'I would do it for any one of you kids.' To which I said, 'The others wouldn't run you into the ground and kill you.' I can't believe the change in her." The elder of Amy's two brothers, a forty-eight-year-old chemist, is also shocked by Ron's selfishness but only complains to her about it. "I've given up thinking he would help; he's good on talk, slow on action," said his disappointed sister.

The last time Amy saw Ron was the day after their father died last year. "I was at the house and offered to help my mother with the cleaning. I remember the exact thing that happened: There were two empty Pez containers on the top of the refrigerator. I asked what I should do with them, and she said to pitch them. My sister-in-law sees them in the garbage and wigs out at my brother, and he screams at me. I walked out and haven't spoken to him since." Seeing her brother take orders from his wife in his mother's house was the last straw. "My sister-in-law does nothing to help. She doesn't even like my mother," Amy said bitterly. "They should be under their own roof."

Amy finds Ron's freeloading contemptible, even though she realizes where it comes from. "Of course, his behavior has antecedents," she explained insightfully. "He was the baby, and he was an accident. At age six he wet his bed, and they took him to a therapist. Our parents' marriage fell apart when he was fourteen, and he got caught in the crossfire." Over the years, their mother favored Ron out of guilt, but her indulgence did him no good. His troubled childhood and her misguided attempts to amend it destroyed his work ethic and encouraged a malignant sense of entitlement. "He never applied himself to anything," Amy recalled. "He didn't get a full-time job until he was in his thirties. This situation is a compensation for my brother's whole life."

Despite Ron's problems, he and Amy had a decent relationship until his wife entered the picture. "We got along as children, but he started changing when he met her. He was desperate to marry—he felt she was the best he could do, and he settled." Ron was the one who filled the void his father had left in his mother's life; "she was always enamored of him," Amy said. I asked whether she was angry or jealous that her mother favored Ron over her and that she allowed herself to be taken advantage of. "Yes, I am, but she's an old lady, and I love her to death," Amy responded. I also suggested that since keeping house for her son's family occupies her and reassures her that she is a good mother, Mrs. Kaplan might be unwittingly encouraging them to stay even though she objects. Amy agrees but still cannot tolerate her brother's conduct. "I would not want any child of mine mooching off me and they wouldn't want to—he's showed my children how not to be," she added.

Ron's behavior has virtually destroyed his already rocky relationship with his sister. "At this point I can't even call it a stalemate between us. Even though he was a big part of my life, I cannot speak to him as long as this continues. If I did, it wouldn't solve the problem; this extends beyond him and me. The thing that must change—the only thing that would allow us to mend it—is for him to move out and take responsibility for himself."

The ways that brothers and sisters manage these responsibilities reflect their personalities, their relationships with their parents, and the quality of their sibling bonds. Sibling eldercare covers the spectrum from criminal exploitation—several people whom I interviewed feared that a sibling was stealing from a demented parent—to worthless or unsolicited advice, to collaboration and mutual support. It is easy for siblings to find rationalizations (distance, professional or family obligations) that allow them to avoid participating with a minimum of guilt. All too frequently, the whole family delegates the job to one devoted but unwilling "volunteer." A colleague of mine lives halfway across the country from her parents (the other three children live down the street from them) and has a family and a demanding job of her own, in addition to multiple sclerosis. Still, she flies in monthly to tend to their needs and has done so for years.

Letting somebody else do the heavy lifting is a popular way to wreak unconscious revenge on a parent (and collaterally on a sibling). Judith Clark, a forty-two-year-old photographer, stepped in to tend to her ailing mother because all six of her older brothers were too busy fighting among themselves to contribute. "I was asked separately by two of them to get flowers for her when she was in hospital when I was by her bedside helping her," she told me incredulously. "Whenever my parents get sick, I'm basically an orphan—it's like I'm an only child. All my brothers do is call me for updates. I'm a one-woman service industry." The fact that the brothers were ill treated by their parents is no excuse for saddling their sister with their care.

Another strategy for evening old scores is to try to get a parent's appreciation (and perhaps a larger portion of the assets) at last by doing too much and then berating one's siblings for not doing enough. Fifty-four-year-old acting teacher Mark Daniels admits that his parents favored him over his younger sister Marjorie, whom he describes as "cold, volatile, and therapy-intolerant":

Even when she was a child, she wasn't good at talking things out; it would just lead to screaming. She fought constantly with my mother, who used to call her "Misery"; my father called her "El Craborino." Dealing with her has always been like trying to grab a knife by the blade. When our mother was diagnosed with terminal cancer, Marjorie felt guilty about how bad their relationship had been, so she precipitously moved into my parents' home and scapegoated me for not tending to my mother as diligently as she did. I had a new girlfriend at the time, who was very precious to me because I hadn't had many. My sister was furious if we visited the house and then went to a movie. I had my own ambivalence about my mother, who was domineering like my sister, and a deep aversion to feeling bullied, so it was hard to be there after my sister put herself in charge.

Marjorie seems to have a legitimate grievance against her parents ("She was envious that there were more pictures of me," Mark told me), but instead of addressing her feelings, she uses self-imposed self-sacrifice as a stick to beat her brother.

Not all assistance that one sibling offers another, however expert or heartfelt, is welcome. Even though she is a professional geriatric care manager herself, Janice Thompson had to learn to bite her tongue and let her estranged sister Julie care for their mother as she saw fit because she came to recognize that any help she offered offended Julie's pride. Julie, who was their mother's favorite and had always envied her more successful older sister, moved their dying mother into her house and designated herself as her mother's guardian. Janice did her best to be useful, driving two hours each way every day to visit and spell her sister, but their ancient rivalry made it impossible for Julie to accept any aid this highly skilled and compassionate woman offered, while complaining constantly that Janice was not doing enough. "My sister and I fought the entire time," said Janice, with helpless regret. "Since caregiving is my profession, all my efforts only made her feel really inadequate; I would pop in, and she was stuck. When I figured out what was going on, I apologized. I told her I loved her and would do anything she wanted me to do to support her, but it was beyond repair because there was nothing good between us to begin with."

Childhood rivalry, parental favoritism, and the havoc they wreak are usually implicated in sibling struggles over parent care. Old conflicts are reactivated in myriad ways—when one sibling sabotages the efforts of another, refuses to authorize necessary treatment, fails to honor a parent's wishes to limit treatment, or will not share decision-making with a brother or sister for fear that this will jeopardize his own special position in a parent's affections. Nothing severs siblings as definitively as fights over dying parents, except those over their estates.

No one who met David and Stan Singer (the siblings whose demented and vision-impaired father was still driving) in middle age—David, a novelist, is fifty-five, and his brother, a law professor, is sixty-one—could imagine that these men, so different in expression, attitude, and even in the way they dress, were close and mutually admiring as children, at least superficially. David attracts the spotlight while Stan recedes from it. The younger brother is witty, talkative, and psychologically minded; the elder one wry, laconic, and unreflective. Both are successful, but David's career has been more public, and Stan's more lucrative.

The lifelong rivalry that Mr. and Mrs. Singer fomented and helped perpetuate between their sons grew out of their own needs for admiration; for years it intensified beneath the surface. Although Stan and David remained civil, mutual envy eventually estranged them, and their lingering resentments discouraged them from trying to repair the damage. As a result, they could not cooperate when the time came for them to care for their parents. Their increasingly tense exchanges troubled David, who struggled to understand their history in order to figure out why his brother had become a subtly antagonistic, closed-off stranger.

The pattern of unhealthy preference, he realized, started early on. "There must always have been competition between us which our parents somehow engendered without knowing it. My mother said she had planned us to be six years apart to be fair; she assumed we wouldn't compete because we wouldn't be attending the same schools simultaneously. That was supposed to solve the problem, but of course it didn't."

The real cause of their later ill will was that right from the beginning each son had been blatantly favored by the parent whose temperament his own most resembled. "I liked my brother when we were boys," David recalled wistfully. "We had fun together—we had neighbors who had two sons exactly our ages, and we'd play soldiers in teams against each other. That was on the surface. But my brother's personality was more like my father's and mine like my mother's. My father and brother were athletic, and we were musical; my mother was a musical star and an outstanding student. The two of them were more restrained and less temperamental than my mother and I; we both have a hysterical edge—we have to be center of attention, and we're good at making sure that happens." Over time, each parent came to ignore the other's chosen son; this seemed perfectly natural.

The star quality of his brother, and how their mother gravitated to him, was not lost on Stan. "She spent more time with me, took me to music lessons long after he stopped taking them," David said. She was also his most enthusiastic audience. "I read her things I wrote—I'd written fiction since I was a little kid. And then I had a freakish success as a teenager, when a short story of mine was published in an anthology and I got paid for it. My mother was ecstatic because it was a good reflection on her. She'd tell me the compliments people told her about me"—in front of Stan. As is always the case, the object of her adoration didn't notice how his unadored brother must have felt.

At first, it seemed as though Stan had joined the fan club of which his mother was president. "On my sixteenth birthday he wrote me a letter from college saying how proud he was to be my brother," David recalled. "It was over the top—he said I could be a Tolstoy or a Faulkner. It makes me embarrassed to think about it; I'm ashamed to be put on a pedestal like that." But Mrs. Singer was thrilled. "She was so moved by the letter, thought it was so wonderful, so eloquent. He compared me to two of the greatest writers ever. It was absurd, like telling some student council president 'You're going to be Lincoln or Churchill.'" Even though David also admired Stan and sought to emulate him ("I thought he was the coolest thing, and I had to go to the same university he did"), he had won a victory that his brother would never forgive. To add insult to injury, David got even higher honors than Stan did at the same college—even though they didn't attend simultaneously.

The bitter envy that Stan had buried for over forty years broke out at their mother's funeral. "Stan said that when he cleaned out her papers there was a closet full of clippings by me and about me and only a shoebox of his stuff. It was so painful I tried to erase it, and shocking too. I felt it's not my fault—what am I supposed to do, hide under a rock? I actually did those things." Guilt over his mother's excessive adulation made him defensive and blinded him to the actual source of discord, which was not his accomplishments but their mother's adoration of them. When I asked why he hadn't responded to Stan at the time, he said, "I didn't feel it would do any good, and I have a fear of saying too much or saying the wrong thing. I'm afraid of sounding arrogant, especially with him. I could be honest with my editor, but not with my brother." This, too, disappeared under the surface.

Ultimately, it was Stan's children who made him his mother's favorite and dethroned his brother; once again their mother's over-the-top partiality deepened the rift between them. "When Stan named his daughter after my mother it was like a revolution," David observed. "Suddenly I was the odd one out. They saw Stan's family constantly and never visited us, and that drove more of a wedge between my brother and me." Years later, their entrenched dueling resentments ensured that they could never work together when their parents needed them.

By the time the elder Singers' health began to fail, the brothers had been quietly on the outs for two decades. "We'd speak twice a year max and only send formal presents, birthday and Christmas cards. Our parents had almost everything to do with it, then and now," David said, his usual sparkle muted when he discussed his strained relationship with his brother. Mrs. Singer became ill first, and her husband, mired in denial, handled her care incompetently. David, who informed himself thoroughly about his mother's illness, was distressed by her needless suffering and the inadequate treatment she received as she was dying. Had the brothers presented a united front, they might have been able to intervene, but Stan, who kept himself ignorant of the severity of her condition, conceded all decision-making to their father, and David could not counter him alone.

Soon after his mother died, David noticed ominous signs that his father's judgment was impaired, and alerted his brother, who once again refused to believe that anything was amiss— a position he resolutely maintained over the years as Mr. Singer became increasingly incapacitated. Every time David insisted on taking an action, such as hiring an aide or moving their father to an assisted living facility, Stan did his passive-aggressive best to interfere. "Stan resented the things I had to do for Dad—we disagreed about practically everything," David said bitterly.

Why, I wondered, did brothers who had once been friends allow competition over their parents to ruin their original goodwill? "We could have talked about it, but then we would have had to talk," David replied with an ironic laugh. "Talking was not used in my family as a means of communication. It served other functions of course—such as the erecting of emotional barriers." Envy and rivalry, and especially unfair advantage, are hard to admit even for people who communicate frankly with each other; for those who never have, the topic is unapproachable.

Even after David arranged, over his brother's furious objections, to prevent Mr. Singer from driving, Stan continued to deny the severity of his father's condition. "He sent Dad alone on a long plane trip, and he got horribly lost," David recounted, still incredulous at his brother's dangerous obliviousness. He prides himself on overcoming his family's childish attitude toward medical matters and blames his brother for perpetuating the family pathology. "Like my father, my brother never goes to doctors and doesn't know how to deal with illness, whereas my wife and I make it our business to learn. Stan feels he should take the lead but doesn't admit I'm suddenly the expert again. He's left everything to me, using the excuse that he was always traveling on business. Here I am all over again with the closet full of stuff, only now it's not filled with a kid's achievements, but with knowledge and expertise about the world. He's envious that I'm younger but more worldly in this area."

Stan's resistance and abdication of responsibility for his father's care have significantly lessened the chances that he and David will ever mend their relationship. "It probably won't happen," David acknowledged. "I'd have to initiate it, but it would have to be a low-temperature thing. It's hard for me to imagine wanting to spend a lot of time with him—he would have to want it, too." I asked him why recovering this bond didn't seem to be worth the effort. "There's probably too much mutual anger—his at me for being preferred by my mother all those years, mine at his good innings thanks to his kids and having more of Dad's attention his whole life. Each of them prevented us from having the other parent and also each other. It was a zero-sum game in my family. I can't change it now."

⁜

As difficult as it is to assure that a declining parent gets proper care when you are obstructed by a passive-aggressive lawyer/ brother, it becomes impossible when your sibling adversary is a recalcitrant doctor himself. Sibling competition is at its most lethal around a parent's deathbed; the barriers to communication that parents set up among their children tend to outlive them.

Tina Cartright's three siblings—her brother Jonathan is two years older, and she has a younger sister and brother— have stopped talking to her because they believe she tried to kill their mother. They refused to allow her to ride to the funeral in the same car with them or to participate in the service. On her part, she has never forgiven them for interfering with carrying out their mother's express wishes and prolonging her suffering for their own selfish reasons.

"Our situation was in the making for a long time," said this sharp and funny fifty-nine-year-old hospital administrator. "My mother and father needed to have a special role with each of us, particularly with Jonathan and me. It was ordained for him to be a doctor and for me to marry a rich guy, both of which happened. The younger two always felt they were in our shadow. Rather than make a cohesive group of siblings, they turned us against each other." Like the Singers, Mr. and Mrs. Cartright's own need to be the center of attention undermined their children's relationships; in a culture of deprivation and favoritism, everybody fends for himself.

Tina's role as her mother's assistant and confidante, an assignment she carried out faithfully to the last, became a fundamental aspect of her identity. "My mother and I always did the dishes and nobody ever helped," she told me. "At holiday meals I would clean up after fifteen people while they all sat in the living room by the fire. Even when they were grown up they were all so selfish—they always felt they should be waited on, like kids. She would say, 'Leave them alone,' but I couldn't let her do it by herself; I didn't want to be a child, too." Tina felt a moral imperative not to permit her mother to be taken advantage of, even when her mother herself tolerated it.

There was a sad contrast in the way her two parents died, and naturally Tina was the one who cared for both of them. Her father, who succumbed first, had an easier time, but there were intimations that her elder brother would cause problems later. "My father had a good death," she recalled. "He went to the gym, collapsed, was diagnosed with multiple cancers, and died within a week. I got the nurse to give him morphine; my brother wouldn't do it. Then my mother got lung cancer and wanted to refuse treatment—she was a member of the Hemlock Society. But she felt she needed to do radiation for my siblings; she was afraid to let them down." Tina's mother was too passive and masochistic to defy her other children's wishes, even in the matter of her own life.

Tina found her mother's agony unbearable as her illness progressed, although, like David Singer's brother, her siblings managed to deny it. "I'd never seen my mother cry, but she couldn't stand the pain. My younger sister and brother lived near her in the same city—I lived four hours' drive away—and nobody was feeding her. They'd go to football games; they were acting like nothing was wrong while she was getting weaker and weaker. I called Jonathan, who also lived out of town, and told him that he needed to come, but he said he was busy and sent his wife."

At this point Tina took matters into her own hands, got a leave from her job, and moved into her mother's house. "I was getting her medications and cooking for her. I'd sleep with her when she was frightened," said this capable, compassionate woman. But her siblings, feeling displaced and overlooked, resented her presence. Sometimes they even ate the food she made for her mother. "They kept wanting me to leave, and I kept putting it off," she said. "Now there is food and company and she's not alone; I was holding a mirror up to them. They wanted to be in charge but didn't do anything, and they got mad at me for usurping the role."

As their mother's symptoms worsened, Tina's siblings grew increasingly suspicious of their sister's motives and pressured her to leave the care to them, while in fact providing none. "They kept saying, 'What are you doing here? You're up to no good,'" Tina recounted. "My sister said, 'We'll all figure it out together when it's time to put her somewhere,' but I said, 'You don't have to put her anywhere; this is what she wants.' Their solution was procrastination and denial. This is my family; they don't talk with you, but they talk about you. They try to manipulate; they don't confer." Her mother's needs, not her siblings' anxieties, were what mattered most to her.

Tina came to her mother's aid one terrible night. "I was left alone with her when she was in such desperate pain that I didn't know what to do. When the doctor finally came, she asked him to give her a shot so she could end her life then. He couldn't do that, but he arranged for medication to ease her so she would die within a couple of days." The rest of the siblings were horrified when they showed up. "They felt I'd talked her into it, but she had made her wishes known to everyone. I said it was up to her, not us; she knew what she wanted. I felt very close to her. None of them would listen." Jonathan even implied that she had killed their father.

Finally, the other siblings were galvanized into action, though not on their mother's behalf. "They barricaded the door so I couldn't get into her room. My sister jumped into her bed to 'protect' her, and Jonathan took her off the medication. He wanted her to wake up so he could talk to her—even though she had told me that she didn't want to, that she wanted to die, and I was following her wishes. He should have come to see her long before. All three of them insisted on withholding medication, and as a result her death took weeks instead of days. They prolonged her agony against her will."

Everybody turned on Tina. She was ostracized at the funeral and not mentioned in the eulogy. Since 2004 she has neither seen nor heard from any of them. "It's a relief not having them stick needles in me," she admitted. "Jonathan is the only one I miss since he's a good man and we were close once, but he's gone."

I asked Tina what role her parents had played in this debacle. "I used to think that because everybody felt like the favorite they must have done a good job, but after they died I realized that really good parents don't split their kids up," she said. "My father was totally domineering, and Jonathan could do no wrong in his eyes. My mother's own mother died when she was eight and she wanted to be best friends with me—if I was talking to one of them, she'd call me downstairs to break it up and have me to herself." Children who are designated parents or companions by their own parents are divided against themselves and cannot stand together.

⁘

Family crises rarely bring out the best in contentious siblings, but occasionally there is a shining exception, in which an obnoxious, seemingly thoughtless brother or sister rises to the occasion, displaying depths of decency and responsibility he or she never seemed to possess before. Their newly admiring, grateful siblings can hardly believe the change.

Doug Sawyer, the fifty-year-old restaurateur who resisted family pressure to hire his arrogant older brother, was moved and astonished by how this same brother behaved when their parents went seriously downhill. Nothing in their previous history could have predicted how faithfully and selflessly he tended them. His actions transformed the future for his brothers and himself.

Joel, now fifty-three, has always been the least-favored sibling in his family; the competition was impossible to beat: Doug and Seth, two darling, tractable identical twin younger brothers who met their narcissistic mother's needs better than he could. The contrast between Joel and Doug, whose warm hospitality and personal charm make his trattoria so appealing, is especially striking; Joel exudes superiority and self-involvement and seems constantly on the make. "Being the eldest and being outranked by twins created animosity that got expressed through the years as hostility toward the two of us," Doug explained. "The rivalry was so intense when we were children. As twins we constantly ganged up on him. Joel developed a very, very different personality than Seth and I. Because his character is much more crude and aggressive, he became very independent; he didn't want to deal with us. He is much smarter than we are, but also a misfit, with very few friends and no social graces." Doug speaks of his elder brother almost as an object in his way rather than a person. "He was something alien in our lives— the connection between my twin brother and me was so intense that we couldn't tolerate that there was this other entity interfering with our inseparable bond."

Financial circumstances had forced Doug to share Joel's apartment for a year when he was in college, and it was such an aversive experience that they stopped speaking while they were roommates and entirely avoided each other for a year afterward. "I took care of the apartment, and he was always there with one girlfriend or another, leaving a mess," Doug told me. "We had a complete falling out." Joel was hardly the kind of person likely to deal with the far more onerous duties of parental care.

And yet, when a series of strokes and cognitive problems debilitated first their father and then their mother, Joel was there. To the twins' astonishment, he was eager to do his part, eventually shouldering the major share of caretaking—dealing with finances, arranging aides, watching over them with commendable patience and loyalty. "In any other circumstances I'd never have anything to do with a person like him; I'd avoid him," Doug said, still marveling at his brother's turnaround. "However, we're bound together because of our parents. And he's doing something I never imagined—he has stepped up to the plate in the time of need."

Joel's help both amazed and relieved Doug, who had been doing most of the work on his own, to the detriment of his own health, until his older brother offered his services. "I did my tour of duty. I took it upon myself to be the designated driver because I'm not married and Seth has a family," he said. "Joel's always been an airhead and I was the stable one—why should I get this shitty job? But then he was available and willing to take them on." I asked what accounted for this change of heart. "Guilt certainly played a role, but also his moral sense; he's definitely a conservative person underneath, and it's a conservative value. We are making reparation to each other; we're getting back together. I can tolerate him now. My aunt always says that our family feuds at breakfast and at dinner they're all sitting at the same table—it's a good trait."

Joel's assistance and the attitude with which he provides it have changed his role in the family, as well as his brother's opinion of his character, for the better. "Before this compassionate side revealed itself, I felt that my parents' death would be the end of our ever having to see each other," Doug said. "Now it will be cordial—there is an understanding that exists between us." The former disruptive "entity" has become a real—if still annoying—brother.

II. Wills and Estates: Poisoned Legacies

The way Joan Bergman's brothers dealt with their parents' will gave her quite a shock. This acquaintance of mine had been the principal caretaker for both her parents as they became old and ill, one with congestive heart failure, the other with Parkinson's disease. As the fifty-five-year-old unmarried sister, and the only one living in the same city, the job "naturally" fell to her, despite her full-time career as an English professor. Joan resented how her parents' needs took over her life, but that did not prevent her from dedicating herself to them for years. She came whenever they called no matter what time it was, spent untold hours at doctors' offices and emergency rooms, held bedside vigils, hired and supervised staff, tried to console and relieve them any way she could. She was the only one of the children who was present when each of them died.

Soon after the second funeral, the siblings read the will. They discovered that it was worded in such a way that the estate, which was considerable, was not to be divided among the three of them alone as they had always assumed, but that the five grandchildren were to be given equal shares, making an eight-way, instead of a three-way, split. This distribution, which their flawed but devoted parents had made without thinking through the consequences, would clearly be an advantage to the brothers, who both had families, but would deprive their sister of security for her future.

Joan's brothers spoke up without hesitation. "We're not abiding by the will," they told her. "We can't do this. You took care of them and we didn't; one-third of everything belongs to you." "Even though both of them could have used the money, they would never let anything come between us," she said, deeply moved. "The one thing my parents did right was to ensure that we loved each other."

Her story, unfortunately, is not the norm. These are the only siblings I know of who made it their business to neutralize a thoughtless act of their parents because they understood that their bond with their sister and her well-being were more important than the bottom line.

☩

Money = Love is a very old equation, one that is played out with a vengeance in siblings' fights over the terms of their parents' wills and the distribution of their possessions. The compulsion to demonstrate, in court if necessary, that you really were your parents' favorite (or to compensate for the fact that you were not) underlies these battles as much as greed does, and blinds people to the consequences, which almost always include the permanent loss of their siblings' goodwill. A lawyer friend told me that even divorces are less rancorous. He described a case in which three brothers and a sister—none of whom needed the money—fought viciously over who should rightfully inherit their mother's jewelry, which was worth less than $25,000. Ultimately, after much time and expense, the paltry spoils that remained were divided four ways by a judge, but the vengeance the suit unleashed destroyed the plaintiffs' ability to be civil to one another or their families for all time. Even if you win a fight like that, you are guaranteed to lose.

⁘

The family home, a deeply symbolic repository of memories and grievances, figures prominently in sibling versus sibling battles over inheritances, even when the "winner" has no intention of ever living there again. I never heard anyone speak with more bitter hatred and terrible disappointment than the three people who told me how a brother or sister had stolen or destroyed family property that should have been equitably distributed among all the children. In each case, the sibling's act felt more like the desecration and obliteration of a precious heritage, and of family feeling, than the mere theft of property. Parents who give this asset to only one child, or who, like Solomon offering to split the baby in half, decree that all the siblings are to own it collectively, bequeath enmity to the next generation.

Dramatic to the last, Todd Riggio's dying mother ordered
him and his two brothers to her bedside to hear an announcement she intentionally kept mysterious: "I need to see you all
and you must be there. I'm gonna say what I'm gonna say, and
then you have to leave immediately because I fear violence."
Even though they suspected what she planned to tell them,
the brothers were not prepared for the full brunt of it. "By
then we'd figured out that she was going to cut us out of the
will," said Todd, an intense and clever fifty-three-year-old
history teacher who is the middle brother, "but when we got
there, she said, 'I have never worried about any of you, but I always knew there was something wrong with your sister, Linda;
I've always feared that she would end up on the street, and
I've spent much of my life trying to protect her. I'm leaving
everything to Linda.' We all said, 'What a wonderful idea;
we'll accept this and even help Linda.' At which point she
scowled like a witch and said, 'Stay away from Linda,' who
was hiding upstairs. Then my mother thanked us, and we pub-
licly reconciled with Linda, but we were lying. I was overcome
by the moment."

I asked Todd whether his mother's fears were justified. "My
reaction was that this was complete shit—she's married to a
man who makes a very good living. This plan was not a last-
minute impulse of my mother's; the two of them had been
conspiring for months." Linda's future was in fact secure, and
her personality, while self-centered and explosive, was more
criminal than mentally ill.

Soon enough Mrs. Riggio's sons discovered that "everything" included the family home, which they had actually constructed themselves decades earlier under their long-dead father's direction. "My younger brother Charlie was the executor of my mother's will, but when he called the lawyer to check on something, he was told he was no longer the executor, that he'd been replaced by Linda. He'd never been informed of the change. Then they put the house we'd grown up in and largely built on the market without telling us—we were scattered all over the country, so nobody was there to see the 'For Sale' sign. My mother did this, and Linda was her accessory," Todd said. With almost biblical cunning, mother and daughter had colluded to rob the brothers of the fruit of their labor. Linda became $500,000 richer as a result.

Todd waited until after the funeral to speak his mind. Linda's insouciance when he confronted her confirmed his opinion that she was crazy like a fox. "That night I sat down with Linda and said, 'I wanted Mom's passing to be easy, but I deeply resent you for accepting this bequest.' I told her that the worst part was how she lied to us. 'I never spoke a lie,' she said. 'But you were part of the conspiracy to do all this stuff in secret,' I said. And she says, 'That's not lying.' Then I said, 'Your brothers would never have allowed our mother to do this to you, and you should make it right.'" His demand, of course, fell on deaf ears.

Linda firmly believed she had God on her side, which mattered a great deal in this pious Catholic family. "She told me that she'd asked a priest about it, and he told her she had the duty of obedience to her mother. In retrospect, Linda prepared very well for not being impinged on by her conscience. She said, 'Your mother made a decision, and I think you should trust your mother.' No normal person could say that sentence."

What could have caused Mrs. Riggio to obliterate and disown her sons for the sake of her daughter? Todd said that his mother identified Linda with her own emotionally volatile and unstable sister, who eventually became mentally incapacitated; making sure Linda did not suffer a similar fate obsessed her. "My perception as a young teenager was that my mother indulged Linda's every nascent semi-demi-quaver of an emotion to keep her from throwing fits, which my aunt was prone to do," he said. Although Todd had been close to both his mother and his sister as a boy, he turned away from them when he saw how badly his mother treated his brothers ("It was all-out nuclear war," he said), while shamelessly favoring Linda. "I concluded that my mother was self-absorbed and destructive and that she didn't play fair. There was no outward break, but I stopped trusting her. I switched my allegiance in the family, changing sides from the axis that included my mother and sister to the other of my father and brothers." The male/female divide in the Riggio household has persisted ever since.

Mrs. Riggio came to merge her identity with Linda's and behaved as though she only had one child. "Eventually, they moved in together; they both wanted to set up a family just for the women," Todd observed astringently. The only good effect of his mother's preference for females was that she loved Todd's little daughter. "I turned back to her to some extent after my daughter was born because my mother doted on her and I loved seeing them together," he said. Todd was able to retrieve some maternal tenderness secondhand. That his mother then disregarded her granddaughter's future heightened his sense of betrayal.

When her children grew up, Mrs. Riggio continued to side reflexively with her daughter against her sons. "My mother exiled me from the family for a year because Linda came to my house to stay for a few days and got into a shouting match with my wife—both of them have tempers," Todd recalled. "I told Linda to leave because she was responsible. My mother called, and I was hoping she would help straighten them out, but instead she said, 'You won't be welcome in my home until you apologize to your sister.' It enraged me that she blamed my wife and me instead of Linda when she hadn't witnessed what actually happened."

In the two years since the funeral, Todd has neither spoken to his sister nor attended any family gathering where she was present. "I see no way to resolve this," he told me. "I don't know how to reconcile with somebody who doesn't think there's anything to reconcile on her side." And yet he yearns to put an end to his family's habit of feuding, which goes back several generations; his mother died estranged from her identical twin, and his paternal grandmother refused to see her own daughter for fifty years. "I've decided not to avoid these occasions anymore; I don't want my daughter to ask me ten years from now why we never see Aunt Linda." He will go for his daughter's sake, not his sister's.

But Todd draws the line at visiting Linda's house, which she purchased and then renovated—twice—at huge expense, funded by the estate. He cannot bring himself to do it, despite the advice of another priest who almost seems to be in cahoots with his sister's spiritual advisor. "My confessor said, 'I'm telling you what you must do: You must have dinner with your sister and tell her how happy you are that she was blessed by your mother in this way,'" he said incredulously. "I thought, what am I supposed to do, admire the house she bought with my daughter's college fund?" In this case Todd answers to a higher authority—his own sense of justice.

The most important reason, though, that Tom cannot conceive of allowing his sister into his life ever again is the fundamental fact of who and what she is. "The problem with reconciliation is, what you get in exchange," he explained. "You get a relationship with Linda."

⁙

At least the Riggio brothers suspected the truth long before they were called to their mother's deathbed; to suddenly discover that a mother from whom you were not so dramatically estranged has left the family home to your brother and cut you off without a cent comes as a sickening shock. Few sibling relationships that are problematic to begin with can withstand so irreversible a demonstration that a parent rejects one child and favors the other, and the heir's untroubled acceptance of the tainted legacy removes any possibility of healing the damage.

Jake Enright was one of those problem children whose parents ignored his disruptive behavior and forced his sister to tolerate it as well. "My brother had an eating disorder," Jake's younger sister, Elaine, recalled. "My first memory of him was sitting at the table having dinner with our monogrammed paper napkins—we were such a cool and proper family—and he'd rip up the napkins, make them into balls, and throw them under the table, while nobody said a word. I have no memories of good conversations. He probably had an antisocial personality—he was a loner and still is—but my parents never had him diagnosed and never sent him to therapy."

Jake's misbehavior and his parents' nonresponse to it were not confined to the dinner table. Elaine said, "He menaced me and chased me around, and he'd go from being a bully to wanting to be friends. I didn't trust him because I never knew who was going to wake up the next morning. My mother's job has always been to protect him and make sure he never noticed anything, just like her. Now he's fifty-eight and has never paid his own bills, even though he has a law degree—I really don't know whether he's working at all." Elaine's mother never thought that her daughter might be in need of protection as well.

The way the Enrights, especially Mrs. Enright, ignored how Jake treated his sister seemed disturbingly like preference, and it left Elaine feeling invisible in her family, an experience this expressive, self-aware, fifty-six-year-old public radio producer still struggles to combat. "My choices were impossible—not to see what was going on or to constantly note and point things out," she explained. "Neither felt ok." The route she eventually took, one that did not endear her to her mother, was to become a whistle-blower. Only when dealing with her brother does she still find herself reverting to her mother's preferred role of the "don't-rock-the-boat/go-along placator."

When Mrs. Enright died six months ago, Elaine had not spoken to Jake in nine years and even skipped going home for the holidays to avoid him. She recalled the "surreal" experience of having to spend the last twenty-two hours of her mother's life in his unwelcome company: "He's on one side of her bed making sarcastic remarks—this is his way to go through the world—and I'm on the other side trying to help her die as she wanted, to have a good parting, with my mother in the middle." Jake's odd, disruptive behavior persisted even when they planned the funeral. "While everybody sat in the front hallway, he began expounding on techniques for playing the guitar. It was so bizarre. I realized that the rest of the extended family is putting up with this, so I interrupt and say, 'Can we work on the obituary?' and get shot down for it. I could not bear watching him act the part of the flamboyant renaissance man at a time like that; it appalled and horrified and repelled me." Her brother's troubling narcissism and the family's tolerance of it evoked her childhood misery all over again.

Soon afterward Elaine discovered that Mrs. Enright had left "everything"—all the family property and the house where Elaine had lived since age six—to Jake; the daughter who tried to ease her dying mother's way and remember her after her death was disowned in favor of the son who thought only of himself. Elaine had always believed that her mother preferred Jake, but her will demonstrated it beyond a doubt. "Her role in making us distanced became clear to me," Elaine declared. A responsible, truly loving parent would have sought legal advice and made an equitable division of assets, perhaps with a special needs trust if she deemed Jake unable, rather than simply unwilling, to support himself. She also would have informed her daughter. Instead, she created an unbreachable barrier between her children.

I asked Elaine why her mother had done it. She believes it was a punishment for pursuing her own independent life. "Six years ago I remarried and moved away from the town where she lived and where I'd taken care of her—I'd gotten her milk from the grocery and run errands for her. Leaving her was unforgivable; I got crossed off every list," she explained with a bitter laugh. "Still, I was surprised at the depth of her unkindness, the lengths she went to. I think she'd planned it all along after my father, who was a fair man, died." As was the case for Todd Riggio, premeditated unfairness by a parent hurts the most because it retroactively ruins any closeness you may have felt.

Elaine has seen her brother only once since she learned the contents of the will. It happened three weeks before we spoke. "Jake said through the lawyer that I could come by the house, my family home, and take a last look. As I drove up the driveway, I could feel the power he still had over me; when I get within his sphere of energy, I don't like who I am. Interestingly, the only things I wanted to take were things that nobody else had wanted." Still, family ties tugged at her. "As I was leaving I was overcome by the thought that I wanted to give him a hug. I did it, and I said, 'I'm sorry it ended this way—it's not what I would have wanted.' He completely misinterpreted me and thought I was literally referring to my disapproval of the work he'd had done on the house. I looked at him and thought, 'This is my brother; this is a person in pain.'" Despite her compassion at the end, Elaine knew that for her own well-being, this meeting had to be their last.

⚜

Even if fathers and mothers do not make only one child the heir to the family real estate, they can still set the stage for strife by leaving it jointly to all their children. I was even told of a case in which the parents combined the worst of both choices by first convening a meeting with their three sons (their two daughters were neither invited nor considered as heirs) and then informing them that they were planning to leave the family home to all three but that the youngest son would have "the right of first refusal" because "he loved it the most," which of course meant that they loved him the most. Like family business partnerships, such emotionally loaded inheritances are sure to cause trouble or to exacerbate fault lines that already exist.

Randy Richardson's father stipulated in his will that his four children were to share the family vacation home in rural New Hampshire. But after he died, Greg, the eldest and the first-born son, immediately appointed himself sibling-in-charge and behaved as though it belonged exclusively to him. Then he did something far more shocking: He committed arboricide on the wild, beautiful property surrounding it. His younger brother, Randy, was appalled. "Greg killed any possibility of a relation-ship between us when he killed those trees," said the sixty-one-year-old, pony-tailed woodworker/artist and nature lover.

"We inherited the place seven years ago," this clear-sighted, forthright man explained. "And we were all part owners, which was a problem to begin with; my father was the glue and tether that kept us civil." At the end of his life, Mr. Richardson con-sidered selling the property and splitting the profits among his two sons and two daughters, but despite evidence to the contrary, he let himself be persuaded that they were, in Randy's words, "mature enough to work it out."

Randy, the youngest in the family, is the only one who lives nearby, and his life differs radically from his more conventional siblings'. ("I'm the black sheep, but a good black sheep," he said in his pithy fashion. "I grew up in the quintessential WASP family, and I didn't become a stockbroker.") Although he is still emotionally involved, he distances himself from the place and from his sibling co-owners as much as he can. "It's old and has a lot of memories in it—my grandparents built the house in 1918," he said, "but my wife and children and I were never particularly welcome there."

On his own authority, Greg had been unnecessarily tidying up the premises by "cutting and trimming" the trees in their woods for years. According to Randy, "That used to piss my father off, too, but he never said anything. This time it was much more violent—he hired somebody to do it and charged all of us the six thousand dollar bill. Money has always been a weapon of control in my family."

Greg did not stop at chopping down trees; without consulting the others, he also desecrated their father's grave by spraying the potent insecticide Roundup over the moss-covered family plot that Randy had carefully tended. "He didn't like the natural moss, so he replaced it all with rocks; he's a butcher," Randy said, his outrage unabated. "His position is always 'I'll do what I want to do, I don't care, and I have every right to do it.' He's one of those people who thinks he can do something now and apologize later but always forgets to apologize or that he's done anything." The violations of nature Greg perpetrated on a landscape dear to Randy's heart ("I'm most comfortable in the woods; that is my place," he told me) hurt him far more than stealing money would have done. His brother's actions proved toxic to their relationship as well as to the vegetation.

Unlike his siblings, Randy had anticipated the problems that sharing the property would provoke among them and tried to take preventive measures. "I wanted to establish rules about who used it when and how decisions were made, but they refused because nobody saw the need. If everybody had admitted the truth, we could have dealt with it, but they couldn't because we're supposed to be a happy family." Greg stepped into the vacuum and followed his inclinations ("He's always believed in primogeniture," Randy remarked).

Greg's motive for redecorating the gravesite went far beyond esthetics. Randy's loving attention to his father's resting place represented the relationship the two of them had finally been able to establish when his father was dying and Randy had tended him. "At the end of his life, my father got upset with the way the family behaved—I'd been such an outsider in my siblings' eyes—and my position with him changed. I made a big effort to help him. I wasn't aware at the time how difficult that was for them. I didn't feel smug about it, particularly since one of things I don't like about myself when I'm around my family is that I feel demanding— wanting to be acknowledged, wanting to be loved, wanting to be seen. Taking care of my father was a moment in my life that was about letting go of that story, but only my father acknowledged it."

The moss memorial represented Randy's new bond with his father, who was also at home in the woods. Unable to share paternal love, the only legacy that mattered, Greg destroyed the evidence out of envy, and the others went along.

Until his father recognized Randy's worth at the eleventh hour, he felt invisible and unappreciated, which made him withdraw and rebel. "I didn't talk until age five because it didn't seem worthwhile," he recalled. "To express emotion or dissent was not ok, and to be outside of expectation was not ok. I wasn't quick-witted like the others, so I spent most of my time alone in the woods." Randy's role as the family outcast makes his eventual reconciliation with his father all the more meaningful and his brother's actions more devastating.

Historically, Greg's and Randy's lives had barely intersected, and nothing good happened between them when they did. "To refer to him as 'my brother' seems more loving than I feel," Randy admitted. "I can count on one hand the number of times I've seen him in the last forty years. He went to prep school at fourteen when I was seven. I hardly remember him from my childhood—either I block it out or there wasn't much." Brotherly love was always in short supply; Greg had assumed the role of the family enforcer years ago. "All he has ever done is tell me what to do: 'When are you going to grow up and get a real job? Can't you discipline your children? How come you're such a disappointment to our father?' There was never a dialogue. I felt that my father told him to try to make me come to the house by myself because he thought my children didn't shake hands properly. Why be around this?"

It surprised me to learn that Greg, who styled himself the scion of the family, acted as his father's mouthpiece, and judged

Randy so harshly, had been no stockbroker himself. When I asked about Greg's profession, Randy laughed contemptuously, as siblings of the shiftless often do. "That's unclear—he hasn't had a job for years, so I don't really know. My sister who still talks to him says he's always mentioning a deal that's about to come through but never does. Nobody's really sure; I think my mother mostly supported him." Greg's was a case of the not-so-white sheep calling the black sheep black.

Over the years since his father's death and his brother's usurpation of the old house, Randy has found a way to manage both his brother and his own feelings about the situation. "My brother is a selfish, arrogant, narcissistic person," said Randy. "I can't be around him—there's too much to cut through. I still have a strong aversion to authority and being told what to do. I still react internally to his demanding e-mails, but now I don't write back with 'Fuck You' the way I used to. When he recently gave me instructions about how to close up the house for the winter, which I've been doing for years, I simply said I'd do it." Randy no longer feels compelled to act out the role of the outcast because he has become a proud and mature man who has gone his own way and knows his own mind. Still, he longs for a real family. "All the same, at some level it all seems so silly, so stupid, and so petty," he said. "I would love to feel that we could do this much better and not go back to the baggage."

I asked Randy how he would feel if Greg died. "I actually thought of that when he got cancer last summer. I wrote him, and there was some acknowledgment on his part," he said.

Even though Randy has no desire ever to see his brother again and has not forgiven him, he has not completely written him off because he knows they are connected.

Randy told me about a wise dream of his that revealed the meaning of the fights over the house and taught him the healthiest way to manage them. His interpretation of this dream reflected his profound self-knowledge about the meaning of sibling strife. "It was wonderful," he said. "I went back to the house, and every member of my family was there, including my ex-wife. I liked that all those people were there and were part of me." "Which part of you is your brother?" I asked him. "The arrogant self-righteous part of me—I've got that part, that I-want-to-be-right part. I know those places in me," he said without hesitation. "I feel no self-reproach about it because if I see something in somebody else that I can't stand, it's got to be part of me. I have to find it in myself." Understanding his inner Greg allows him to deal with the actual one.

Ultimately, what has enabled Randy to disengage and even recognize his kinship with the brother he despises, who destroyed the place he loved? Instead of fighting with Greg and perpetuating the family dynamic, he has literally moved on and created a place all his own, while maintaining a nominal role in the old family house. "I can let go of their house; I've built another little cabin in the woods. That's my house with my family," Randy said with a proud smile in his voice. "I really love my life and how I'm living it."

As Esau knew, living well by having enough—and building a home of your own—is the best revenge.

CHAPTER 8

IRRECONCILABLE DIFFERENCES

Sibling Relationships Beyond Repair

⁙

For the final five years of my brother's life we had no contact; my going through the motions—typically at my
mother's urging—stopped in 1999. The last time I saw him,
I brought him a present for his fifty-ninth birthday. That was
one of very few times I ever went to his apartment, although
it was a ten-minute drive from our house, where my mother
still lived and where I stayed when I visited her. I had racked
my brain to find a gift that from the little I knew about him
I thought he would enjoy: *The Buena Vista Social Club* CD,
which featured an evocative solo on trumpet, the instrument
he played professionally. He'd had a leg amputated from the
diabetes that was ravaging him, and I knew that music was
his chief consolation, as it was mine. He unwrapped the
package, putting it aside without looking at the contents or
thanking me, and said abruptly, "I'm a disabled person. I need
help—I need money."

I was taken aback. This plea sounded like a well-rehearsed pitch, so impersonal he didn't even call me by name; I also knew that his living expenses were provided for by disability insurance and that he had access to services for the disabled. Feeling rebuffed and turned off—was I nothing but an ATM?—I mumbled something about needing to use it to take care of our mother, who had dementia, and left as fast as I could. Later I wrote him that money was the one thing I could not give him, but the letter went unanswered. We never exchanged another word.

But we had one more potent interaction several years later, through an intermediary, that unnerved me. In the middle of a session with a patient, I got a telephone call from a social worker in the emergency room at a hospital in my hometown. "Is this Steven Safer's sister?" the voice said. The question, which I don't recall ever being asked by anybody before, seemed strange. "Your brother has just been admitted in cardiac distress. He's unconscious now, and I need your permission as next of kin to operate on him to install a pacemaker." Our biological relationship, the only indelible connection we had left in the eyes of the world, had put me in the position of deciding whether my brother would live or die—and I had absolutely no idea what he wanted.

Having been told that I had a few minutes to decide, in a state of shock I struggled to figure out the right thing to do. As soon as my patient left, I called the social worker back. Had my brother said anything when he was brought in that could help me intuit his wishes? Did she have any impressions? She told me that he had said something like "I guess I'll have to go through this." I could hear the tone of stoic resignation he would have used; you don't forget your brother's voice. "Operate," I said.

The next day I called her again. To my relief, Steven had survived the surgery and was coherent. I told her that I needed more information if I would ever be required to make such a decision for him in the future, that he had to talk to me and make his wishes known, explicitly and directly. I had to force his hand; I could not endure ever being put in that position again. I held the receiver while she went to his room and asked him if he would talk to me. "He said no," she reported. Somehow, I had still hoped to get through; this was the end. "Remove me as his emergency contact," I responded. It was a small comfort to know that the decision to refuse the only service left for me to perform for him had been his.

⁙

I haven't known him for years, and I don't want to know him; there's nothing there for me.   —DAVID SINGER

In some way she feels dead to me already.   —BONNIE SHORE

We fought all the time from an early age. . . . I can't get through an hour's visit with her.   —DEBORAH ANDERSON

To refer to him as "my brother" seems more loving than I feel.
—RANDY RICHARDSON

I dread when she calls.   —NANCY CAMERON

The problem with reconciliation is, what you get in exchange: You get a relationship with Linda.   —TODD RIGGIO

People sound similar when they talk about a severed sibling relationship, regardless of what went wrong. Their voices become flat, hopeless, bitter, or cold, as mine used to do, but there is usually sorrow underneath; the prospect of the other person's death troubles them, even if they have no intention of ever meeting again. The language they use to describe the sibling is overwhelmingly critical—"arrogant," "nasty," "empty," and "stupid" are typical adjectives. Most of these people have a long history of trying to work it out and have made numerous attempts to get closer that have been rebuffed. Usually there was some last straw, an act of cruelty or supreme selfishness, that made the relationship deteriorate until further contact became impossible or had to be kept perennially at a bare minimum. Almost always, however, even between brothers and sisters who have not spoken to each other for decades, pain persists.

Estrangement is a state of mind, an emotional even more than a physical distancing. Many siblings who consider themselves estranged (the euphemism "not close" is also popular) from a brother or sister continue to have contact out of guilt, a sense of family solidarity, or an unwillingness to make a definitive break. Cutting your closest relative out of your life for good is rarely simple; it usually happens only after repeated efforts at rapprochement have gone nowhere.

All estranged siblings feel a lack of ease or intimacy in the other's presence; they never regard the person as a friend or confidante, someone they miss or turn to in times of joy or sorrow. The degree of estrangement depends on how much contact they are willing to tolerate, but, surprisingly, it is not always fixed in stone; life circumstances can cause unanticipated fluctuations.

I. Six Degrees of Sibling Separation

1. Total, permanent alienation

The relationship is over or it never began. These siblings have severed all contact via any medium for a long time and have no desire to reconsider; they reflexively avoid attending any function at which the other will be present. The sibling has been excised—at least consciously—from their lives.

2. Obligatory meetings only

Wedding-and-funeral siblings initiate no personal contact. They see each other only on "state" occasions and then only when other family members act as a buffer. Meetings are tense at best, overtly hostile at worst.

3. Going through the motions

These siblings keep contact at a minimum. In addition to attending family occasions, they exchange birthday gifts and Christmas cards but avoid one-to-one interaction as much as possible. Neither enemies nor friends, they maintain the pretense of cordiality but never anticipate meeting with pleasure.

4. Cool civility

Both parties occasionally initiate contact (e-mail is ideal for this purpose) and tolerate each other's company, but intimacy is lacking and avoidance is entrenched. Problems are never discussed. Each may have the wish to improve the relationship, but neither is willing to make the major effort it would entail.

5. Rapprochement by proxy

Children and spouses are the medium through which these siblings tentatively approach each other initially. There is distance and discomfort, but both parties have the desire for more satisfying contact, although it is rarely expressed directly.

6. Chinks in the armor

These siblings have a history of serious strife, but life events (aging parents, the birth of children, illness, or personal growth) have led to more appreciation and moments of mutual goodwill that make them want more warmth or believe that goodwill is possible between them.

✢

Sheila Wagner's combative relationship with her older sister, Karen, was doomed from the start; ten years' difference in their ages did nothing to quell their constant fighting. Since they are distant relatives of mine, I remember the atmosphere of chaos and hostility in their house on visits during my childhood, but I never knew the source of their flagrant strife until Sheila and I talked about it when she was fifty-eight.

"Karen is a bit of a witch," Sheila said. "We never got along." Their mother virtually guaranteed their enmity by creating a literal physical barrier between her children: "She put a gate like you'd use for a dog across my sister's room so I couldn't get in there because she felt it was unfair for a toddler to interfere with a teenager's life; she'd had a much younger sister who got all the attention." Knowing that she could get away with it, Karen used to torment Sheila by stealing her stuffed animals and putting them in her own room, where Sheila could not retrieve them. As usual, a retrospective attempt to right a childhood wrong ended up causing the original victim to commit a complementary one as a parent herself later on and—also as usual—to be blind to the impact on her own children. As a result, even through Sheila became her father's favorite ("I was the smart one," she said proudly), she has felt rejected by her mother all her life.

Karen did not fare so well; being her mother's favorite did not cushion her from either emotional or physical woes. "She was always writing me letters in the middle of the night. She suffered from insomnia when she was in college and dropped out after one year," Sheila recalled, which suggested that there was at least a brief time when the sisters were not enemies. "She was in and out of hospitals for three years with colitis. From the outside her marriage looked good, but she never loved her first husband. Then she married a short, fat, stupid guy and abandoned her own children. It was such a selfish thing to walk out like that, and I was kind of saddled with her three daughters, whom I didn't like—I called them 'The Coven'—it wasn't nice of me." Despite her unabashed contempt, there was a catch in Sheila's throat when she described her sister's misfortunes and her own unkindness.

Sheila stopped speaking to her sister twenty years ago after Karen's second husband yelled at their dying father and refused to apologize; this was the final straw in a relationship that had long been on the skids. "From then on I refused to see her when she visited our mother; once somebody crosses the line, they're out," she explained. I had the feeling she had been looking for an excuse to sever it.

Only when Karen almost died in an automobile accident did Sheila call her, and even then, she claims, "it was only out of guilt." Randy Richardson acted similarly when his detested older brother the tree-killer got cancer, and many estranged siblings I know in New York City got calls after 9/11. It is one thing to choose to dissociate yourself from an unsavory sibling, but the prospect of an involuntary separation through death compels you to acknowledge the connection even if you repudiate it the rest of the time.

Relief, contempt, and bitterness do not prevent Sheila from feeling sorry about her sister's fate and about the impossibility of any bond between them; it is a rare sibling who does not feel such regret. "Now she's fat and very unhappy," she said with more pain in her voice than I expected to hear. "She was a pretty, pretty girl, and she threw it all away. When

I read books about siblings with good relationships, I'm jealous, even though I'm closer to my cousins than I've ever been to her. I wish I'd had a mother, too, so I've made sure to have a good relationship with all my own children." Her eldest and youngest are twenty years apart, but she has seen to it that they are friendly. Sometimes, even though the past is beyond repair, you can avoid making the mirror image of the same mistakes your mother made, and spare the next generation.

The prospect of total estrangement affects every sibling differently. Sheila Wagner, who welcomed it and even arranged it because she found her sister so noxious that she saw no point in continuing contact, is at one end of the spectrum; others have more nuanced, even ambivalent, reactions. Elaine Enright, who avoided her brother for years yet spontaneously hugged him at their final encounter on the driveway of their childhood home, considered the split necessary for her well-being but regretted losing her only remaining family member ("We are siblings; we are linked; we share a last name," she said sorrowfully). Bonnie Shore has no illusions about the possibility of normality with the sister who had a violent tantrum at their mother's funeral ("You can't have a sisterly relationship with an active volcano," she asserted), but she still gingerly attends family functions so as not to cut her off entirely.

There are also siblings at the other extreme, who feel compelled to keep trying to connect with difficult brothers and sisters even when regularly rebuffed because the pain of a final separation feels too great to bear. Against all odds, their efforts continue long past the point where most people would have given up. When they finally accept the inevitable and begin to mourn their losses, they feel no relief, only resignation and sorrow.

Jackie Johnson's strenuous efforts to maintain affectionate bonds with her elusive brothers were probably doomed from the start. "I don't speak to either one—but I try," said this frank and open fifty-one-year-old minister, with a quiet sob. Her twin brother, Matthew, a factory worker, was a dyslexic delinquent who got caught robbing newsstands at age ten and later was dishonorably discharged from the army for his pathological lying. That he eventually joined a politically and religiously conservative Evangelical church—his sister heads a liberal Christian congregation—made it no easier to find common ground. "We're like two ships passing," she said.

There was a brief period of camaraderie when Matthew had a baby. "We could be together around her, but when she grew up it didn't last; she's faded away," Jackie told me. "He and I really don't know what to talk about. After my mother died, we never saw each other; my mother was the hub. It's terribly painful for me."

Jackie, now herself the mother of twin girls, is hungry for family. When her efforts to align with her twin failed, she attempted to establish more rapport with her older brother, Mark, a doctor who became a Buddhist. Even though he made sexual overtures to her as a teenager and never apologized, she pursued him, undaunted by his alcoholism and unwillingness to engage. "I've tried to see through all that," she said. "I long for company and connection. I asked him to go to therapy with me, and he said no. He said, 'I want to be there for you,' but he never has been. I'm out of his sight and out of his mind. I still want his approval. I keep hoping he'll turn into somebody I can relate to—I want an older brother." As Jackie described her tireless efforts to make both these unresponsive men genuinely fraternal, the phrases "I try," "I'm at a loss," and "I don't know what to do" recurred repeatedly. Her sense of helplessness is palpable.

The atmosphere in the Johnson family was hardly conducive to sibling solidarity. Their father was a philandering clergyman who tried to beat his younger son into submission ("I took Matthew's side when he got whipped, but he never trusted me—I feel sad talking about it," she said) but did not spare the rod with his other children either. "My mother and I were more deeply connected, because I was the only girl; the boys only had Dad. I got better, sweeter protection than they did," she explained. Both brothers still envy and resent her.

Jackie was the only one of her siblings at their mother's deathbed. "I begged Mark to come and he said he couldn't. Matthew wasn't there either—he thought she loved me more. Her dying wish was that the three of us would get back together and love each other; she saw us separate, and it broke her heart." The desire to honor her mother's request, and her own religious faith, increased Jackie's fervor to mend the rift among them.

Jackie has pursued insight and self-knowledge as intensively as she has pursued a bond with her brothers, with far more success. "I've had twelve years of intensive therapy—

I take good care of myself and my soul," she said, adding, "I don't want to judge, but I don't think they do." Although Mark's unstable personal life troubles her ("He's been successful monetarily, but he's had a series of relationships that didn't work out"), her unbridgeable distance from Matthew is even harder to endure. "He's five minutes younger than me," she noted, emphasizing their intimate biological connection. "We've never had a horrible fight. He probably thinks I don't want to be with him. He's a good guy with a big heart, but he needs therapy to work through his lying. He's shut down. I sense he's pretty lonely." Her daughters also want their uncle, a twin like them, in their lives ("For some odd reason they like him," she noted ironically), but even they cannot get through to him, which is another source of rejection for Jackie. Fortunately, she has had the foresight to bring other men into their lives to replace the brothers who have forsaken her: "I've sought brothers elsewhere. I've created a wonderful surrogate family and uncles for my girls; they feel deeply heard."

Right before she and I spoke, Jackie had made what may have been her last-ditch effort at détente. "I sent Matthew a birthday card and I just invited both of them for Thanksgiving. My twin didn't respond—I rarely hear back from him—he insists he's really busy. Mark said he'll probably be on call. I can't do it anymore." A tone of bitter finality momentarily crept into her voice. "You see the fucking *Brady Bunch* and *Leave It to Beaver*, and you want a clean, wholesome, loving family." I had the sense that she was facing reality, but she had to force herself to do it.

I asked Jackie how she would feel if she and her brothers were to die unreconciled. "I would feel unfinished because of all these years that we haven't been together," she said. "But I wouldn't feel regret because I've worked to try to open the door that they kept closing—my sorrow would be that death would be the final closing."

Although her brothers have decisively shut themselves away from her (barring unforeseen circumstances), she has wisely decided not to terminate her internal relationship with them but to understand it more deeply; this is the only aspect of their kinship that is in her hands. "I ask, 'Who are they in me?' she said insightfully. Her affinity with her twin is the first thing she is addressing because it is naturally deeper and probably more difficult. But even as she confronts their disturbing similarities, she also makes a distinction between the two of them, another sign of healthy self-esteem. "Like Matthew, I've also had problems with exaggerating, out of my own need to be accepted and seen as good; he was an outrageous liar. I can also relate to his rigidity about religion—that is so tied into what I left behind. Twenty years ago when he embraced it, he hoped that would be the way we would find each other again, but I have changed. He is a lost part of me. What can I do? With both of them now it's a matter of letting go, of grieving and letting go."

The desire for reconciliation and the efforts to bring it about must be mutual to be effective. There is a limit to what even the most determined, loving heart can accomplish all alone.

II. Seven Rules for Sibling Disengagement

1. Breaking up is hard to do

Deciding to terminate contact with a sibling, or accepting that estrangement is already a fait accompli, is a difficult emotional task because it always evokes childhood pain. Don't minimize it; recognize it and work it through.

2. Giving up hope can be good for you

Despite our fantasies about families, just because somebody is biologically related to you doesn't mean that a healthy relationship is possible. Brotherhood and sisterhood should be earned.

3. Sibling estrangement always involves loss

Losing even the most noxious sibling hurts because family is our foundation. Grieving for what you never had is as important as grieving for something you have lost.

4. Things can change

Estrangement is rarely static; experience alters people for better and for worse. Sibling bonds are deeper and more complicated than they appear and can be revisited over time, with surprising results.

5. Siblings are indelible

Even if you never want to see the person again, a sibling is forever part of you and your history. Severing your external relationship doesn't mean that you can divest yourself of the internal relationship. It cannot be severed as long as you live and will reveal itself unexpectedly.

6. It takes two

There is no such thing as unilateral reconciliation with a sibling, except within the self. Even with the best will in the world and repeated efforts, love cannot be created or resurrected by one person's desire. Sometimes you must seek family elsewhere.

7. Make a choice

Whatever decision you make about the type of relationship you will have with a problem sibling, make it a conscious choice; you will have fewer regrets later on. Avoiding the painful truth, blaming external circumstances, letting the relationship trail off, or believing it no longer matters prevents recognition, resolution, and mourning. Acknowledging reality liberates emotional energy, and this will help you discover men and women who can become your authentic psychological brothers and sisters even if they are not your biological ones.

CHAPTER 9

FRIENDS AT LAST

Reconciliation

⚜

I interviewed only one person who actually experienced a scene of reconciliation with a sibling as it is portrayed in fiction. She was still basking in the glow when she described it to me. "My older brother was horrible to me as a child, but he's a good guy now. For the longest time I didn't know that I could hang up the phone when he harangued me, and ten years ago I finally told him he couldn't do it anymore. Earlier this year, he called me weeping; it was a movie moment. He's open to the fact that he could be a total jerk; he's done a lot of work on himself. Now I adore him, and I never thought I would say that. It's one thing to recognize that somebody hurt you, but to have the person say it and really know he did is miraculous. I realize it won't be a smooth road, but now we're doing it together. His call was a gift, a diamond I walk around with."

Their encounter was memorable for its sincerity, and its rar-
ity; after a lifetime of strife—Carol Mann is now forty-five
and her brother Fred is fifty-seven—things almost never get
resolved so completely. But after even this ideal reconciliation, Carol realistically anticipates bumps along the way. Now
they are engaged in the real task, rebuilding their relationship
from the ground up, that their hard-won and well-deserved
mutual goodwill makes possible.

What this brother and sister accomplished epitomizes the
scenario that all siblings have to follow, explicitly or implicitly, in order to make up in an authentic and lasting way. One
person, usually the more insightful sibling, initiates the dialogue. In this case, Carol took the first step by putting Fred
on notice that he could no longer victimize her; by confronting
him, she transformed herself from a victim into an active par-
ticipant and declared herself his equal. Even though he could
not respond immediately, Fred heard what his sister said. Then
he took the essential steps of examining himself, holding himself accountable for his behavior, and communicating with
her. Carol also "did a lot of work"; even though Fred had been
the aggressor, she made the effort to grasp the tragic circumstances that had made him so cruel and controlling. "Our
mother assigned him to be the dad since my dad, who was an
obese alcoholic, drowned," she told me. Understanding how
her brother must have felt to be thrust into such a role helped
her to empathize and be open to his heartfelt apology. Their
complementary actions set the stage for what followed. Carol

concluded by telling me, "Now we're doing it together." An ongoing dialogue became possible because each sibling strove to see the world through the other's eyes.

Reconciliation, the recovery of sisterly and brotherly love— or at very least the ability to tolerate being in the same room— is a powerful, precious, and life-changing experience; it can even alter the way you interpret the past. As in estrangement, there are degrees of reconciliation, ranging from no longer hating and totally avoiding each other to becoming intimate friends. And, also as in estrangement, life experience causes fluctuations in the degree of forgiveness and fondness siblings feel. Although all acts of rapprochement after years of alienation have fundamental elements in common, they unfold in as many ways as there are relationships to be restored. Sometimes not a word is uttered, sometimes it happens at a deathbed or after the sibling has died, and in one case I witnessed, a posthumous act of reunion was actually arranged by a dying person. Things you resignedly thought were written in stone can yield something new at any time and in ways you never imagined.

I. Deeds, Not Words

Anna Ross and her older brother, Josh, are good friends whose personalities are quite different. Their families take joint vacations. He praises and admires her, and she appreciates his excellent qualities, even though they are interlaced with difficult ones.

When they were children left alone together because their mother was working, Josh locked Anna outside in freezing weather without a coat, punched her in the mouth and broke her teeth, and once even kicked her between her legs with pointed shoes until she bled. Together, over the years, they worked through these horrors, "with no forgiving requested or granted but definitely there."

"I was at Josh's mercy, totally unprotected by my parents," Anna told me, with a certain intensity in her voice as she recalled her suffering. She is a fifty-two-year-old documentary filmmaker, and Josh, a dentist, is five years her senior. "His psychological cruelty was almost worse than the physical abuse—he was hyperactive, but nobody called it that, and he was never diagnosed, even though our father was a psychologist. He really needed authority. At age thirteen they sent him to boot camp in the summer, and he came back a changed person, completely calm. He knew that the last episode between us was awful and over the line, but we never talked about it."

Even though he never lost his abrasive edge, Josh's subsequent behavior conveyed his remorse, and he has been the one to pursue their relationship. "He grew up to be a decent and good human being," his sister said. "He's still a little insensitive, but he's a good dentist; he does favors and gives to charity. Strangely enough, he's been the one who was very concerned about family relationships and keeping it going. His desire was definitely there: Let's reconcile and be siblings again. I have to hand it to him because I, Ms. Family Values, was ready to write him off."

I was curious how she came to trust and appreciate him in the absence of any kind of formal acknowledgment, which most people assume is a prerequisite for recovery from such a childhood. "He did make a few glancing and humorous references to things he did—like 'I gave you a hard time, but you turned out so well.' Abuse was just part of our relationship. There must have been good things in addition to the terrible ones; I managed to integrate it somehow. Lots of therapy helped me understand my parents' role—that was absolutely essential."

Another essential factor was that Anna came to empathize with Josh's tormented childhood, and her generous spirit allowed her to appreciate what he was able to do to make amends. "Knowing how socially awkward he was, for me his picking up the phone was saying it all—that was admitting that he was in the wrong; I read a lot into it. There have been other times in my life when people haven't acknowledged the wrong they did, when they just took the step of reengagement. I knew that this was his acknowledgment, that that's what it's gonna be. He's done something big; I accepted it. He had grown up, really grown up, and I saw that. I was not afraid of him anymore. Since then we've had many happy times together—there are still painful outbursts occasionally, but I could see he'd changed and he really felt something." In Anna's case, seeing was believing, and it gave her brother back to her.

II. Death Opens His Eyes

Crusty, loquacious eighty-three-year-old psychiatrist Dr. Lenny Brown gave plenty of reasons why he and his younger sister Sandra had barely spoken for twenty-five years: She was an alcoholic at one point; she had a schizophrenic son and a lesbian daughter; she married a "Mafioso type" and they moved far away; she fought bitterly with their aging mother when the mother moved in with him. "People drift," the lifetime socialist and self-proclaimed "rationalist" explained. "It wasn't comfortable. I'm not superior at having relationships. I had all I could handle in my own life and in my practice caring for the poor and downtrodden." The real, devastating explanation emerged only slowly, when they finally discussed their past as she lay dying.

Sandra was seventy-one and gravely ill with a cancerous tumor in her back when she saw her brother for the last time. "I went there, and we finally got everything out," Lenny said. The cause of their rift turned out to be something that—astonishingly—had not occurred to him before that moment. "I didn't think of this: My parents had left an inheritance, and I was the executor. It partly got spent and partly got stolen. That drove us apart." I noticed that he used the passive voice as a way both to deny responsibility and to obscure the ugly truth that he had squandered her share. "She was very bitter and wanted to know what had happened. I told her openly about the losses in detail—I had a failing restaurant that I was trying to keep afloat—and that seemed to satisfy her."

Why, I wondered, had he not told her before? "It never came up; she never asked" was his explanation; for him to take the initiative would be to admit behavior hardly befitting his self-image as the defender of the downtrodden. Even when we spoke about it years after the fact, this highly intelligent man could not bear to admit the obvious: "I've tried to reconstruct it—did I steal something? Did I do something wrong? What I did wrong was not keep her informed, but I never had a sense that I was holding back. I was very involved with myself. We were in a pretty bad crisis: We declared bankruptcy; we were going to lose our house to foreclosure."

Something in Lenny's manner must have expressed authentic contrition even though his words did not because Sandra responded by recalling a tender memory. "Then she said to me, in her daughter's presence, that I had been her best friend when she was younger." Her announcement brought back the incident so vividly that he switched to the present tense as he recounted it: "Now I remember! She's been stood up by a date at a dance; she calls me, and I'm ready to kill the guy on her behalf—and I'm not a violent person." He started crying softly and speaking haltingly, his bravado gone. "A lot of sadness, we'd fallen apart. That probably could have been said if I were a different person. I never took it up with her at all— yeah, there were things I could have done. I'm very regretful about the whole loss and really shaken when she says I'd been her best friend." It genuinely grieved Lenny that Sandra still cherished the time when he came through for her, even though he failed her miserably later.

When Lenny finally told the truth to his sister and himself, memories of their old rapport came flooding back and insight followed. Sandra, he remembered, had admired and emulated him. "We were very friendly when she was in college. She did the same things I had done—she even became a psychiatric social worker." Admitting his guilt also allowed him to recognize and to regret, for the first time in his life, that their parents' blatant preference for him had sowed the seeds of entitlement in him and bitterness between them. "We'd come from a very privileged background, all kinds of fancy stuff, upstairs and downstairs maids," he said. But Sandra, he now saw, went unnoticed in the midst of the luxury. "Nothing was ever right between her and my mother. My sister felt I was an only child. In our house there were two portraits done by an artist, one of my mother and one of me, great big paintings, four by six feet," he said with shame and sorrow at his blindness. His presence loomed large in the house, but Sandra had not merited a portrait. "You don't comprehend what's going on—whatever part of the brain looks at itself doesn't look at that. I'm sorry I screwed up." Despite his defensively convoluted language, his pain was palpable.

Sandra and Lenny were deprived by fate from building on what they had rediscovered. "What happened after you confessed to her?" I asked. "Nothing," he said bleakly. But I didn't believe him; I wondered whether he felt any closer to her. "Only in my head," he said, as if that didn't count. "It was very near the end. *Wasted*." He uttered the word like a self-laceration and a

cry of despair. "Both of you were kept apart by silence," I observed, feeling far more sympathetic toward him now than I
had started out. "And for somebody who talks so much," he
added, with bitter self-knowledge and a flash of ironic wit.

In the end, Lenny, who for decades had eluded responsibility for his criminal selfishness, punished himself for failing
to appreciate how he had changed as a result of their meeting.
When I asked what impact seeing his sister again had had on
his life, he was silent. Finally, he said, "I feel a lot more humility. When I see patients, I'm more sensitive and more kind."
He has also cultivated a relationship with Sandra's daughter,
who now spends holidays with her uncle's family. Talking
frankly and unsparingly about his follies proved he was telling
the unvarnished truth.

Sandra, who died ten years ago, is no longer cut off from
his thoughts, and his regrets still haunt him. "I think about
her from time to time, and I wish I'd been close, particularly
as people I know drop off. Now I remember how protective
of her I used to feel." Then he told me the final, generous
brotherly service he performed for her. "I was very sad when I
saw her suffering. Before I left, she kicked everyone else out of
the room, and we discussed my obtaining morphine for her
for assisted suicide. She asked me to do it, and I agreed. Fortunately, she died before she needed it. We really got very close
very quickly again—I guess it was still there, for if it was gone,
it wouldn't have come back like that. I was moved. I regret so
much." At the end, he came through for her again.

III. Death Opens Her Eyes

We naturally assume that the survivor is the principal beneficiary of reconnecting with a dying sibling. But when I interviewed Eve Redfield, a sixty-nine-year-old former teacher and
a devotee of the female Indian mystic Gurumayi, in the last
months of her life, I saw that laying the groundwork for a
posthumous reconciliation can transform the dying one as well.

Although Eve apologized in advance that her pain medication might interfere with her thinking clearly, her mind
was sharp, and her tongue was sharper. Her eyes were sunken,
and she used supplementary oxygen as she sat at the kitchen
table of her childhood home, but this compact woman's directness and clarity were, if anything, intensified by her situation. "I'm dying because I had to stop chemotherapy," she
said unflinchingly. "I couldn't tolerate it without taking natural remedies, which my brother, who's in charge of the family money, refuses to pay for."

How could one sibling be so heartless that he could deny
the other more than just her share of an inheritance, but life itself? "Abe and I have no relationship at all, or if we do it's
contentious. He turns everything around, and in his mind
it's always been me who's doing what he's actually doing," Eve
explained. She then proceeded to narrate a history of mutual
envy, mistrust, miscommunication, and pain, all of which was
originally orchestrated by their oblivious parents and perpet-
uated relentlessly by themselves over more than half a cen-

tury. In a tone that indicated the scores were far from settled, she said, "Abe is three years younger than me. In my mother's mind, he was the perfect one. She was so special herself that there was no room for a special little girl, so there was never any money for what I wanted. But for him there was—he got guitar lessons; I didn't get art lessons. 'Don't even ask; we don't have it' was the message to me." Curiously, she also asserted that "Abe felt tremendous rivalry towards me and was absolutely sure I was the preferred one. He assumed that I was pampered and given all sorts of advantages I wasn't actually given because I was the valedictorian and he didn't do well in school. My father felt tremendously jealous of his younger brother, and that's the model my brother got." For reasons related to their own childhoods, the Redfields behaved in such a way that each of their children concluded that only the other one was loved. Rivalry prevented the siblings from forming a bond.

As a girl, Eve did her best to make her brother pay for his presumed advantages. "I hated him, used to call him names, and did everything in my power to make him miserable, until puberty, when he got stronger and built a moat around himself," she recalled. "I really wanted to have a relationship then and he wouldn't allow it." "Did you apologize for the way you treated him?" I asked. "No," she said; "it never occurred to me." In a family like this, words are used only as weapons, and communication is as alien as self-awareness.

By the time Eve felt remorse and wanted to make amends, the drawbridge was yanked up for life. "In my forties I did try.

I told him how mean I'd been to him when we were children and I couldn't blame him for having felt the way he did, but his response was 'It's always about you.' Everything was my fault; there was no repairing what had been created. At first I wasn't mature enough to do it, and when I could, he would have nothing of it; there was no getting through the barrier." When she saw that the damage was so complete that she could not salvage their relationship, Eve sought a symbolic family elsewhere, eschewing "materialism" and making a pilgrimage to India to become a disciple of her newfound spiritual mother.

Illness often prompts embattled siblings to call a truce, but in this case it only inflamed their conflict. Eve, who was already ill when their mother died, was supposed to inherit the house (she never married, and her brother had a family and home of his own) and receive a portion of the money. She believes that the sum, though small, "would have made it possible to go on working and living." She did get the house, but she said that Abe, echoing the theme of their childhood, "felt he was being cheated, and insisted on dividing the investments in a way that I couldn't function." Since he was prosperous, and the remedies she required were not exorbitantly expensive, his refusal had more to do with grievances than finances.

But by then Eve was too depleted to fight. "He denied that my needs were real; he's why I had to end treatment," she said, resignation in her voice. Of course, they could not discuss their feelings. "I wanted a brother, a closeness, caring, and concern that we'd never had before, but he went on and on about the awful things I supposedly did and what a user I am. He was so aggressive and violently rejecting that there was no room to think." Her hopes that her fatal diagnosis would finally make reconciliation possible were dashed.

In such dire circumstances, why did Eve insist that the brother who consistently rejected her pleas be her sole source of help? Stubbornness, entitlement, and pride—none of which jibed with her religious principles—made her unwilling to seek assistance elsewhere.

The explanation Eve offered for Abe's conduct was a startling mixture of contempt and compassion. "My brother knows how to fight for what he wants and he'll kill. He's not very bright—he made his way to the top of his profession by manipulation and deceit. The blueprint he had for old age didn't include taking care of me. Needing anything from him made me sad because I never wanted to be a burden to him, but when I told him this he didn't believe me. He's terribly resentful and totally materialistic. I don't think he thinks; he just reacts. I have all these great friends who check in on me," she said as the phone rang, "but my brother never does." Then, seemingly unaware of the contradiction, she said, "He did call me once recently and to my surprise I found myself very, very eager to talk to him, but it was just another manipulation, and he went back to being rejecting."

Suddenly, the bitterness left her voice, and she said gently, "I think he's always had to fight, that he's had a dog-eat-dog life. He's materialistic because he's used money to try to buy love. I'm looking at someone who's terrified and lonely. Whatever threatens him, including me, he gets rid of as quickly as possible and is relieved that he survived. He's proud that he's provided for his family, which our parents could not, and that makes him feel powerful, which nobody in our family ever felt. He doesn't want to be identified as my brother because he's embarrassed and confused by my nonmaterialism; that's understandable. It's so sad that we can't give each other affection or protection. He can give those things to his wife and children, though; he's a good father and grandfather. That's why I think he's worthy of being forgiven."

I asked Eve if she had any regrets about their bitter stalemate and was astounded by her response: "No, I don't, because I've decided on a plan to show him I've forgiven him. Even though I have no desire to give him anything, I got inner guidance to leave practically everything, including the house, to him. He doesn't believe me even though I've told him, and he actually witnessed me changing my will. My friends think it's a bad idea because he'll feel guilty, but I believe he'll find a way not to. For me it's a way of trying to heal, to make a last gift, to say, 'Here, I really don't wish you any harm at all.'" The behest, she believes, provides irrefutable evidence of her goodwill—and it has the additional, unconscious benefit of forcing him to acknowledge their kinship. She created the means to achieve after death what she failed to do while she was alive.

Eve's "inner guidance" reveals multiple motives. Her friends are right, of course; she is trying to make Abe feel guilt and remorse for hastening her death and refusing to accept her apologies or her way of life. Even though she sees it as a straightforward gift of forgiveness, her gesture embodies ambivalence—outrage and sympathy both. She wants to hurt him and make peace with him simultaneously. Her behest is a postmortem act of contrition for her old hatred, as well as a declaration of unrequitable love.

IV. She Said/She Said

"I just met a perfect person for you to interview," said a journalist friend who knew I was writing about sibling strife. "She told me that her sister approached her and said, 'I want you to know that this is the first time in my life I didn't feel extreme fear or unbearable rage when you walked into the room.'" Fortunately, both the speaker and the object of this extraordinary declaration were willing to talk to me about what had prompted such an explosion of feeling, and what transpired as a result—a remarkable act of courage and candor, particularly on the part of the sister who had been the aggressor. The accuracy of that sentence turned out to be one of the few aspects of the process they agreed on—proof once more that two people can interpret an experience so differently that it is hard to believe they are talking about the same thing.

Laura Myers, the elder sister and the one to whom the announcement was addressed, admits that her younger sister Kim was "invisible" to her from the day she was born. Laura, now a fifty-two-year-old actuary, claims not to have noticed Kim when she was taken to the hospital to see her new sister in the maternity ward ("I was held up to the window and remember seeing my mother, but not her"). Clearly, Kim's birth was not welcome. For the next six years, during which they shared a bedroom, Laura treated Kim, who is now a forty-eight-year-old publicist, only as an object to torment. Kim, on the other hand, found Laura far too visible. "One of the most psychologically consuming relationships of my life has been with my sister," she told me. What the aggressor erased the victim could not get out of her mind.

Laura may not remember Kim as a person when they were children, but she catalogued in disturbing detail the relentless physical and psychological suffering she inflicted upon her. "Things got abusive," she said at first, employing the passive voice to obscure her guilt as Lenny Brown had done, but then she elaborated: "I felt extreme dislike and resented having her around, so I would do things to torture her. I divided the room in half with masking tape and punished her if she crossed it—the bathroom and the door were on my side. I also used to sit on top of her and tickle her until she told me she loved me. I was a horror as an adolescent; my sister was just the wallpaper." Obliterating her sister's very humanity while insisting on declarations of love added a note of sadism rarely visited on wallpaper; uncontrollable hatred and envy are more accurate descriptions of Laura's feelings than mere dislike and resentment. She must have been acting out intolerable rage and feelings of helplessness. Although Laura admitted that she was "a bossy, unhappy kid" who felt "terribly guilty," she described Kim as a crybaby and an outsider, which was another way to mitigate the severity of her cruelty even as she acknowledged it. "Kim had a different temperament than the rest of family. She was extremely sensitive and cried easily, but she also played it up," she said.

Where were their parents while this sister abuse was going on? "They were in their own worlds," Laura said tartly. "My father was busy protesting the Vietnam War, and my mother was busy with her headaches and solitaire. She was aware but oblivious; she said it made her sad that we didn't get along." Such drastic understatement on their mother's part and the self-involvement of both parents left their daughters without the help they desperately needed.

After the girls got their own rooms, they continued to fight bitterly, often physically, and their enmity persisted even after Laura moved out at seventeen. What Laura identifies as their last blow-up was ostensibly over skis. "We had identical cross-country skis," she recalled. "I lost one of mine and claimed one of hers that she insisted was hers. We yelled at each other. For the only time in my life, I got so angry I was shouting. I was taken aback by her extreme rage at me and by all the stuff that had built up and never got resolved." It struck me that shouting was in fact a more benign expression of anger than her earlier behavior had been and that her shock at her sister's pent-up fury was another indication of how much unconscious shame and anxiety caused her to deny the gravity of what had gone on between them.

Then Laura made a revealing confession. "I realized that the ski was actually hers, but I didn't admit it." When I asked why, she said, "I haven't given it a lot of attention. I had so many other things to talk about in therapy—we place the sibling relationship on the second tier." I noted that she said "we" instead of "I," as if to share the guilt. When you erase your sister, you erase your own feelings as well as hers—and until recently most therapists failed to notice.

Laura's account of how she came to appreciate Kim retains vestiges of denigration along with unusual candor. She openly admitted that her invisible sister became visible to her only by degrees and at first exclusively through the eyes of others. "I remember wondering what her handsome college boyfriend saw in her—could she have qualities I hadn't noticed?" she said, without a trace of irony. "I realized we had the same taste in music when she went to a concert I would have liked; she got it together and she went. At that point I started to see that she was a unique individual; I didn't like her, but I thought she might have positive traits." Finding her sister likable was difficult because it would make it difficult to like herself after she had treated her so brutally. "Kim's happiest years were after I moved out and she got to be the only child and blossomed," Laura said. "I saw that she'd developed without my paying attention. I went to her graduation and I thought, 'Who is this person?' Then I started seeing her life, and we began spending more time together. Now we're close."

Throughout our conversation, Laura had not referred to the exchange that brought her to my attention, so I asked about it. "Kim had the courage to tell me that when I was thirty-two," Laura said. "It opened the opportunity for us to talk about how horrible I was. Now suddenly our relationship was real; we were not just going through the motions—it was a great relief. I was so full of extreme gratitude to her for allowing us to have an honest conversation. Of course, I listened to her experience and completely validated it. I was able to tell her my theory that I was so vulnerable that I took it out on her." When I asked about their current status, she replied, "There's still some rapprochement going on, and tensions of course," tensions she attributes to the disparity of their financial situations. "What has brought us together is discussing our mother. This is something we could bond over. It allowed us to repair our relationship." Kim had not only become fully visible to Laura; she had become audible as well.

I expected Kim to have a different point of view, but I was not prepared for how radically her account would diverge, both in the details and the emotional content. It was unsettling to see that the two sisters had truly experienced alternative realities. Although both were now engaged in reconciling, one felt closure, but the other did not.

Kim continues to feel traumatized by the first six years of her life with Laura and has spent a great deal of time and thought coming to terms with it. "The anxiety hasn't completely gone away," she admitted. "When I look back and try to understand and evaluate, I see that I took a lot of what happened between us at face value. Why didn't I question it? I didn't even realize until young adulthood that I wasn't responsible. I didn't know any different—but my parents must have known; they saw the room." While Laura presented their interaction as strictly sadomasochistic and certainly devoid of fun, Kim's version was far more nuanced, with intimacy and brutality mingled.

"I have tender memories and memories of her boxing me out—there were certain sections of our room I wasn't allowed to be in. But we also used to take baths together and spelled out words with soap on each other's backs, and we'd sing folk songs, trading lyrics back and forth from our beds at night. I idolized her as a young girl. I thought she was the greatest. I loved her hair, her taste in music; I would have reveled in any doting. My emotions are so mixed—that really defines our relationship into the present. We're open enough to talk. The painful parts are residual; that's what I've come to accept."

Kim depicts a more unsettled, conflicted present-day situation than her sister does and as much love as hatred throughout their lives.

That Laura does not remember the good times between them deprives her of her own humanity and makes her seem more consistently mean than she really was. Perhaps acknowledging that they had in fact shared tender moments and that Kim had idealized her and longed for her love would make Laura feel even worse about having mistreated her. In fact, however, it may be the basis on which their reconciliation is being built.

The one thing that both sisters agree on is that Laura's moving out of the house was the best thing that ever happened to Kim. "Things started to get better when we got separate rooms, our own space," she said. "And living there was a lot happier for me after she left." But they remember different last fights (though with the same theme) while they still lived under the same roof, and neither mentions the one the other cites. "There was one instance when she tried to dominate me and I resisted for the first time in my life," Kim told me. "It was so loaded: We were watching TV together on the couch, and she threw her legs over my lap as if to say, 'This is my space and I'll take it.' It was not affectionate. When I pushed her legs off, she put them right back. I tried to force her to remove them, and we scuffled, physically fighting each other—I was defending myself. That was the last time she bullied me. After that, I just resisted when she came back home and tried to retake that role." Laura has no memory—or at least did not report any—of her sister standing up to her because it does not fit into her narrative of their relationship and her view of Kim's character.

Recognizing the full brunt of what Kim had endured came in stages. Unlike Laura, who relied on external evidence to revise her perceptions because she had to disconnect from her emotions, Kim used her own internal responses as a guide. "It wasn't until I was an adult that I ever seriously questioned the way she treated me," she said. "I didn't even realize that it wasn't my fault. I have a very distinct memory that helped me see it differently: I was in my twenties and recently married.

My husband and I were goofing around and I accidently kneed him in the tailbone, and I remembered that she used to do that to me arbitrarily, all in 'play.' I had internalized the notion that this was play, but I suddenly saw that it wasn't normal; you don't hurt someone for fun." Kim also explained her crybaby reputation. "My family has a real ethic of being strong, so my only defense as the younger child was to cry or complain. I was dismissed as too sensitive—still am. They thought I took things too seriously. The message I got was that things weren't so bad." Recognition came only after she no longer lived with her family and was able to reinterpret her experience.

I asked about The Conversation. She was unexpectedly vague about the particulars and far more equivocal about the resolution than her sister had been. "I don't remember exactly what happened or when," Kim reported. "It was during the period that I started exploring family dynamics in therapy. Only then I discovered that my family wasn't the ideal family I'd always imagined. The outcome has never been completely satisfying to me because I don't think Laura's ever really apologized. If I felt some regret from her, it would be different, but instead she told me about how much pain she must have been in as a child to treat me that way. She always talks from an analytical distance—she's figured it out, explained it away, and doesn't even understand what it was like for me. I need some sense of contrition; without that, my ability to trust her is irreparably limited. I have friends who have incredible relationships with their sisters, and it makes me so sad." What Laura considered satisfying closure, Kim saw as incomplete and lacking in the fundamental elements of empathy and re-morse necessary to build a bond between equals, a bond she longs for.

Laura made an error that those who have seriously mis-used a sibling often commit when they try to reconcile: She talked more than she listened. The compulsion to explain comes from defensiveness and the wish to be relieved of intol-erable guilt, but it is often interpreted by the victim as making excuses. Hurt siblings need to be seen and heard, and their experience validated, before they can forgive or even listen to explanations. The aggressor has to offer a heartfelt apology, which can happen only after she faces the truth head-on. But first she must make a serious effort to empathize with the pain her sister has endured and demonstrate that understanding, a heroic undertaking. Short-circuiting this arduous process can damage a precarious connection. Rebuilding trust—or creating it in the first place—takes time and self-examination.

Kim needs more from her sister, but she does give Laura the credit she deserves for acknowledging her childhood cru-elty when Kim confronted her. "She said she abused me," the younger sister said. "That was important; describing our rela-tionship that way helped me see it." Even though I wondered whether much between them would have changed if Kim had not spoken up, for the perpetrator herself to call a spade a spade at long last made her behavior vividly real and was as brave an act as the victim's original declaration.

In the dialogue of reconciliation, both siblings have to take risks. Therefore I suggested to Kim that "another step in your liberation would be to say, 'I'm not sure I trust you; you've never really apologized.'" "It's so hard for her to credit my perspective as equal to hers," she replied. "But if you really considered yourself her equal, your sister would have to do the same," I observed. She gave me an example of how their conversations get stymied. "Once when we tried to talk, I said, 'You're not seeing the situation accurately,' and Laura replied, 'That's not the way it was. I have a master's degree in psychology—I always understand what's going on.'" In this latter-day verbal equivalent of the leg incident, Kim let Laura have the last word, which reinforced the same hierarchy they had in childhood. "I've asked to be relieved of being dominated," Kim said, without realizing that this formulation put power in her sister's hands once more—power that originally traumatized victim and perpetrator alike. Reprogramming so entrenched an interaction takes repeated efforts; Kim cannot keep allowing Laura to stop her in her tracks. Acting like Laura's equal will make Kim feel like one.

If they work at it, the future augurs well for Laura and Kim. They have already achieved more amity than siblings with their history usually do. Kim has an excellent relationship with Laura's son, and the sisters have indeed found common ground by discussing how their mother failed them both. Kim, echoing Laura's words, told me, "My therapist said an enlightening thing to me—that I turned to my sister for mothering, but she couldn't give it to me either. I hadn't realized that's what I really wanted." These motherless children are now discovering genuine commonalities in their lives as adults, despite the residual tension. "My sister and I have similar interests, including human service, and we can talk," Kim said. "I love and admire her, but there is still this dominating dynamic. She often needs to have the last word, to direct the situation. She can't cede the position of authority. On the rare occasions that she does, it's amazing and wonderful. We can have good conversations despite it, but I'm always waiting—will I have to be wary, or will this be a time I can just be who I am?" This is another thing she should say directly to her sister rather than trying to figure it out internally; genuine intimacy must be built on frankness. Kim said, and Laura would agree, "There is enough love and affection that we didn't end up hating each other—it's not perfect, but it's good." Considering where they started, this is progress indeed.

V. Found in Translation

When I first met Dr. Cynthia Greenberg, she was haunted by her childhood hatred for her younger sister Lynn, and desperate to make amends; in this case it was the aggressor who was pursuing her former victim. Cynthia was eager to talk about her predicament in hopes of gaining insights that would help her find a way to approach Lynn, explain herself, beg her sister's forgiveness, and pave the way for the intimacy she longed for. This passionately sincere, self-reflective, forty-four-year-old pediatrician's intense sense of remorse, as well as her hunger to do the right thing, was palpable. But she was terrified of making a wrong move and being rebuffed irreparably. Ironically, in her zeal to take the blame she felt she deserved for freezing Lynn out of her life, she risked committing the same error that Laura Myers did—wanting her sister to take her guilt away rather than working it through on her own.

Cynthia had such a sense of precariousness about her relationship with Lynn that only her urgency to resolve her anguish compelled her to broach the topic with me. "I'm worried that she'll recognize me in your book," she confessed. "I really care about her, and I don't want to make things worse—but the truth is she'd never read anything like this." Lynn, a forty-two-year-old mathematician, is as resolutely rational and uncommunicative about her inner life as her older sister is introspective and voluble about her own. "We are on speaking terms, both very polite," said Cynthia. "But the current status is that I'm the bad one, and I want to burst out of that role. So much of what troubles me is not about any overt conflict but the way I feel about the situation—the struggle takes place inside my body." If only she could make Lynn understand her state of mind, she believes, she could stop tormenting herself.

Like Laura, Cynthia remembered that she too had a viscerally negative reaction to her sister since her birth, but she had no idea what caused it. "When I first went into therapy at age twenty-four, my most serious concern was that we had a terrible relationship, and I wanted to understand why," she recalled. "There was always an awful vibe between us." Unlike Laura, Cynthia never physically tormented her sister, but she did ignore and reject her. "We never fought," she said, "but I hardly acknowledged her existence. I never engaged with her, never reacted to her as if she mattered. It was cold indifference, not overt aggression; I didn't even bother being mean to her." Cynthia spent seven years trying to figure out exactly what could have poisoned their interaction, consolidating information, making deductions, and finally reconstructing the shocking truth.

Her first clue was a photograph that she had known about her whole life without understanding its implications. "My mother has a meticulous photo album, and in it there's a picture of me in a hospital room with the caption 'Meanwhile, Lynn was born.' I knew I'd been a patient at that time, but I started to wonder whether she'd been taken home before I was—maybe I felt replaced by her." She checked her discharge date and discovered she was right. But was sibling rivalry a sufficient explanation for the intensity of her feelings? Being exposed to very young patients during her pediatric rotation in medical school sparked her curiosity, and made her dig even deeper. "I decided to investigate what actually happened when I was a patient myself, so I sent away for my medical records," she said. There, in the handwritten forty-two-year-old chart, she found the answer:

> I was hospitalized for two weeks with a severe bladder infection when I was seventeen months old while my mother was giving birth in the maternity ward. I had horrible, traumatic procedures done on me, and my mother was not allowed to visit me the whole time. When I saw the records, I realized

I'd been left alone in the hospital, and then I came home after fourteen days of horror to find a new baby there. What I
pieced together is that I must have assumed Lynn was the
reason this happened to me. Reading those records was a huge
turning point; my whole life fell into place. I've felt this intense, irrational hatred even as an adult, and I could not shake
it. It was such a blessing to finally know the truth. I was so
overwhelmed that I couldn't even tell my therapist for a
month. Now I understood how I could say I despised Lynn
but I didn't know why—it was because her very existence was
anathema to me.

Excitement and relief were mingled in her voice as she recounted her story. A terrified one-and-a-half-year-old child
alone and in pain, who could not understand even if anyone
had tried to explain what was happening to her, would of
course have blamed her newborn sister for her suffering. Her
parents were otherwise engaged and no help when she came
home. "That it was a nonstory is the worst legacy," she said.
She couldn't wait to tell Lynn.

In her zeal to unburden herself, Cynthia did exactly the
wrong thing first. "I told her everything I had been through
and asked her to have compassion for me," she reported. To
her sister's chagrin, Lynn stonewalled her. "I don't believe that
the things that happen in childhood affect us as adults" was
all she said. Cynthia perceived her error, although she saw no
way to fix it since her sister's blunt answer seemed to preclude

further discussion. "For me to ask her to empathize instantly with me was wrong," she acknowledged. "What I should have done first is to admit that I had been hostile to her all her life and that she must have known it." She also should have explicitly added, "I'm sorry I treated you so badly," because an explanation without an apology risks being interpreted as an excuse.

Cynthia made another mistake that siblings who are attempting to reconcile are prone to: She acted as if she and Lynn spoke the same language. This assumption further alienated Lynn, who shunned the very psychological exploration that her sister embraced. Cynthia believed that what she needed to say was what Lynn needed to hear; in fact it only entrenched the problem and made Lynn feel invisible all over again. Lynn's response was not simply a rejection of Cynthia and her plight; it was an authentic expression of her own personality and point of view. In order to really put the relationship to rights, Cynthia needed to figure out how to reach Lynn on her own terms; she had to see her sister and look through her eyes.

Cynthia knew that Lynn believed—correctly—that their parents preferred their more ebullient, expressive older daughter, but she did not immediately appreciate that Lynn's perception colored their entire interaction. "My sister has made that 'Meanwhile' under her photograph the basis of a lifelong grudge against me," she said. "She's always felt that I've gotten more attention." To Lynn, Cynthia's inopportune confession was just one more example of her hogging the spotlight. When Cynthia finally acknowledged the special position in her family that she took as her due, as favored children will, she began to understand that her initiatives unwittingly reinforced their childhood roles.

Why was Lynn so resolutely antipsychological? Her personality was naturally more retiring, and she had to differentiate herself from her more expressive sister in order not to languish in her shadow. Yet at the same time, Lynn mimicked everything Cynthia did without ever acknowledging it. "She copied me for much of my life," Cynthia told me, with some of her older sister's irritation coming through. "She went to the same boarding school I attended, transferred to the college I went to, majored in the same subject I did—even got married in my redesigned version of our mother's wedding dress." How could Lynn ignore her and imitate her at the same time? "She wanted to be a better version of you to get your mother's attention," I suggested, with the clarity that comes from not being involved in an interaction. Cynthia later told me that this explanation came as a revelation that helped shift her feelings for Lynn from annoyance and incomprehension to compassionate regard and, later, appreciation for her own unique qualities. Another pair of eyes is very useful when you are trying to see a sibling.

When Cynthia and I first spoke, Lynn remained a painful cipher to her even as an adult, impressive though frustratingly alien. "She was a brilliant student, she has excellent judgment, and she's a really good and successful person," Cynthia said. There was genuine appreciation to build on, but she had no idea how to communicate it. They saw each other twice a year, mostly at family holidays. Discussing her failed attempts at reconciliation inspired her to try once more. This time, armed with new insight and hoping that she could express herself more persuasively (as well as more safely) on paper, she drafted a letter to Lynn and sent it to me for comments. Even though it was clearly heartfelt, I encouraged her to make it briefer, simpler, and less confessional—more Lynn's style. She labored long and painstakingly on revisions; it must have felt like her last chance.

But unbeknownst to the tormented letter writer, seismic shifts were already occurring on both sides. "Writing that letter to her changed something for me, though I've yet to send it," Cynthia told me. Then she described a recent weekend, the first in their lives, in which they actually had fun together. "We had a wonderful time," she said excitedly; "it felt surprisingly easy." Their extended family had gotten together to survey nursing homes for the sisters' aging father—a portentous moment for everyone—and had gone out to dinner in a large group afterward. Lynn had been a huge help throughout the process. "I noticed that only she and I were keeping track of what everyone ordered, and I did something I'd never done before: I said, spontaneously, 'You and me, Babe, together we could rule the world.' I appreciated her and felt like myself; we even laughed together." Cynthia, at long last, was noticing

Lynn and telling her playfully how alike they were in the things that mattered most.

Meanwhile, Lynn had also changed. "She had all three of her kids make a valentine for my son, which she brought along. I was very touched. That gesture meant a lot, the second-generation thing," Cynthia said. It was of tremendous importance to both of them.

Nine months after she began her letter to Lynn, Cynthia, still full of trepidation, finally mailed it. She eagerly anticipated seeing Lynn at Christmas and finding her responsive at last. But the course of true reconciliation never does run smooth: "All she said was 'Thank you for sending me the letter—it really wasn't necessary,'" Cynthia reported, crestfallen. "I was so hurt. I felt dumbfounded, deflected, and erased." All her analysis, all her work on herself, seemed in vain. Lynn was rejecting her all over again, slamming the door in her face. Her herculean exertions to reach her sister seemed destined to come to nothing.

She didn't realize that Lynn was speaking the simple truth.

⁂

Six months later when I called to check on their progress, I couldn't believe my ears. I expected at best a polite détente and found instead authentic appreciation on both sides. The desperate urgency, pain, and anger were gone from Cynthia's voice, replaced by tenderness, warmth, and joy. The letter, as

Lynn said, was superfluous because their strife was healed. Through the alchemy of joint effort, they began to bring out the best in each other; they had turned hate into love.

What happened? Cynthia had learned to empathize with her sister, and everything flowed from there. "When you said she was trying to be a better me as a way to get our mother's love, my heart opened to her, and I felt compassion for her for the first time. I felt I could love her; it was so poignant," Cynthia explained. "You also helped me get myself out of that letter—that was a pivotal intervention." The guilty one who had started out seeking compassion for herself ended up feeling it instead for the one she had wronged.

Since we originally spoke, Cynthia had come to recognize that her sister was indeed responding in her own way. Lynn's communications also became easier to read—both clearer and more consistent. The two women will probably never have the deep, soul-searching conversations that Cynthia craves, but she doesn't need to look to Lynn for something that her own more psychologically-minded friends can provide. Sometimes you have to adjust your notion of the perfect reconciliation to the good-enough one that accepts the other person as she is.

At long last, they have become truly visible to each other and have found a way to reach each other. "Now we're coordinating our vacations," Cynthia said, to my astonishment. "We're going to the old family house on the coast so our boys can be together. Her son loves my son—it's so healing, and we both want it so badly." This was the first time I had heard her say the words "we both want" about anything; their relationship had turned into a mutual project. "How do you know she wants it too?" I asked. Cynthia's response showed the depth of her newborn sympathetic understanding. "She does so many thoughtful things. She's very generous; she gave money to a charity I'm active in without telling me." A year earlier, I thought, Lynn's nonannouncement of her donation would have been cause for offense. When we feel secure in another's love, we become less sensitive to potential slights. "She cares for the things I care about—that's how she loves me."

Generous, loving gestures, she had learned, were Lynn's native tongue.

VI. Seven Rules for Sibling Reengagement

1. Making up is hard to do

Any attempted reconciliation is full of false starts, wrong turns, and misunderstandings. Frustration is to be expected. But patience and persistence often pay off—and you'll usually have more than one chance. Listen first; talk later. Assume that you don't really know your sibling. Instead of pursuing an agenda, open a dialogue. You won't know in advance how far it will go or what form it will take. The essential task is learning to recognize your sibling as a separate but equal human being.

2. Work on yourself first

Why do you want to reconcile with this sibling? The motive that has the best chance of success is wanting a better relationship with someone who has an important psychological role in your life. Don't attempt it if your main objective is to meet other people's (your parents' or your spouse's or your therapist's or society's) expectations, or just to assuage your guilt.

3. Take the initiative

Don't wait for your estranged sibling to approach you; make the first move yourself. Being the initiator often pays off. Be frank and clear about your intentions. Tell the person that you know you have grown apart or have never been close and you'd like to try to change that. If you feel there is something worth salvaging, what do you have to lose?

4. Seek a new perspective

Take another look at your sibling and at the family dynamics that led to strife. This is probably the hardest and most important step you can take before approaching your sibling. Ask who your sibling is independent of the relationship with you—as a son or daughter, as a friend, a spouse, a parent, a professional. Who is this person you grew up with, then and now? How did he or she experience your parents? Who was favored? You have to grasp the other's reality to have a chance at changing the relationship between you.

5. Accentuate the positive and seek common ground

You know about your sibling's flaws, but what are his good qualities, admirable character traits, or accomplishments? Does she have strengths that you don't? Do you have anything in common? Do you have any good memories? If so, remind your sibling of them; appreciation builds goodwill.

6. Look through your sibling's eyes

How does the sibling conflict look from the other side? Make the effort to empathize with your estranged sibling. Genuine desire to hear an opposing point of view will register with the other person. You hear and react differently when you understand where somebody is coming from; it humanizes the enemy.

7. Take risks

The truth can hurt. What your sibling has to say will probably be at odds with your good opinion of yourself. Be prepared to be told things you won't like. Be willing to see things from a radically different, sometimes infuriating or critical, point of view. Your willingness to hear, undefensively, how the other person sees the situation establishes trust, which is the most potent tool for reconciliation.

CHAPTER 10

THINKING NEW THOUGHTS
ABOUT SIBLINGS

⚜

The purpose of *Cain's Legacy* is to bring stressful sibling relationships into conscious focus so that their potent, indelible
impact makes more sense. I hope it removes the barriers of
indifference, paralysis, anxiety, or simply not knowing what
to do that prevent us from approaching them with an open
mind. Rifts with brothers and sisters cause pain, and in our
desire to protect ourselves, we avoid thinking about them, to
our detriment.

Things improve only when we make ourselves the agents
of change, and sibling trials are no exception. Thinking (and all
the feelings that accompany deep thought) gives you choices.
When you have choices you are no longer a victim of circumstances; even the most entrenched sibling struggle can look
different from this expanded perspective. New habits of mind

can be cultivated, and self-inquiry is one of the best ways of reconceiving experience; it can be transforming.

I offer the following observations as a way to evoke the mental state in which change can occur, to bring some light into the dark corners of our psyches where such relationships usually lurk. These fundamental principles can help you look with new eyes at yourself and your sibling. They involve altering your perception of yourself vis-à-vis your sibling and altering your perception of your sibling vis-à-vis yourself—the prerequisite, but not the guarantee, of improving the relationship between you.

1. Face the problem

Do not succumb to the ever-popular geographical-proximity fallacy ("We'd get along better if we lived closer to each other") and its many corollaries, the assorted external circumstances that we blame for our psychological distance from difficult siblings. The real problem is always interpersonal and internal and cannot be properly addressed without recognizing its true sources. Any excuse or explanation that leaves emotions and history out of the equation encourages avoidance until it is too late.

2. Realize that difficult siblings follow you everywhere

Take this relationship seriously. It matters more than you think, even if you've had no contact for years. The worse the sibling strife, the bigger the hidden impact it has on your life, and the more it has to teach you about yourself. If you look away, you cut off a unique source of insight—but you can choose to reengage psychically at any time. Your sibling does not have to participate in this part of the process and need not even be alive; your internal relationship with the other person is the essential thing.

3. Understand your parents' role

Strife between brothers and sisters originates in family interactions as well as in the characters of the combatants. Favoritism pits siblings against each other. How parents handle these conflicts largely determines the quality of the bond siblings develop. As an adult, identifying how your parents contributed to the conflict can help you alter it.

4. Resisting change is natural

Transforming an aversive sibling relationship requires a willingness to open old wounds, to challenge protective assumptions, to reconsider the past—all risky, scary, and unsettling things. None of these actions is popular in contemporary society, but the only way out of pain is through it.

5. Accept that you don't really know your sibling

Difficult siblings are strangers who grew up in a different family, live in a different world, and speak a different language than you do—even if you spent your entire childhood together. Your view of them is distorted by anger, longing, hurt, disappointment, or the need to justify yourself, as well as by the fact that you may not have had contact for years. Once you are estranged, the image of the other person becomes fixed in your mind. You and your sibling are stuck with images of each other that may bear little resemblance to the adults you have become; you both may be demonizing a fantasy. Therefore, if anything is to change, you should mistrust your assumptions. Two complementary tasks are necessary to discover a brother or a sister as a real person: looking *at* your sibling and looking *through* your sibling's eyes.

6. Abolish Sibspeak

Real communication is essential. Stop ineffective management strategies such as "keeping it light," and start setting limits and speaking straightforwardly to your brother or sister. Do not allow yourself to be reactive, to tolerate subtle accusations, or to be silenced by the universal fear that acknowledging and addressing the problem will exacerbate it. Bringing conflicts out into the open never actually makes them worse, but colluding in keeping them underground allows them to fester and ties your hands. To admit a problem clearly and directly initiates dialogue, forces you both out of your respective ruts, and fosters reengagement. Avoidance only perpetuates sibling strife.

7. Use every resource

When you're trying to see sibling stasis in a different light, enlist other people—friends, therapists, relatives—who can provide another view of your sister or brother. Input from others, especially from somebody who knows her or him in a different capacity than you do, can reveal sides of your sibling that you may be blind to or that do not come out in your company. Taking yourself out of the equation sharpens your vision, and distance enhances perspective.

8. Think about your motives and goals

Are you engaging in a reclamation project or a research project? Do you want to reconnect with the other person or simply to understand the reasons for your estrangement more deeply? Even though it's impossible to know if you will succeed in reaching your sibling should you decide to try, identifying your intentions can help determine how to proceed. The right course of action is entirely subjective, based on whether you determine that reconstituting this relationship is worth the effort. Is there enough positive feeling for you to rebuild or create a lasting bond? If the person dies while you are estranged, would you feel mostly relieved or indifferent or sad that you never had a real sibling? Or would you feel grief-stricken that you didn't try to fix it and that you might be missing something precious? Coming to terms does not require reconciliation, only reconsideration. Remember that reconciliation is not up to you alone; the effort must be mutual if you are to reenter each other's lives.

9. Siblings can surprise you

And so can your reactions to them. Circumstances you are not privy to can affect how they respond to you. They can seek you out years after you thought the tie was severed forever or revert to bad behavior after a promising rapprochement. They can be receptive when you least expect it or not follow the scenario you have imagined and carefully laid out. Flexibility is essential because you can never be sure how a sibling will behave; rigid expectations and set agendas leave no room for the improvisation that is always a component of the reconciliation process. Fixing a conflicted sibling relationship is always a work in progress. Old hurts leave scars, and making up is just the beginning. Establishing trust and goodwill allows you to work through the problems that will inevitably come up. Both of you deserve second chances.

10. There is no one-size-fits-all solution to sibling strife

There are many different models in *Cain's Legacy*—thoughtful, open-minded severers and sensitive, insightful reconcilers, as well as numerous gradations in between. The outcome is less important than the process. Any good result requires self-examination and rediscovering the human being who is your estranged sibling. Every meaningful solution starts from the same receptive stance: active emotional engagement and searching for insights in your history. The only person whose involvement you can control is yourself, and that is all you need.

✢

I cannot guarantee that your sibling will come back to you even if you follow these recommendations faithfully. But I can promise you that once your eyes are open, you will never want to close them again.

A NOTE
ON SOURCES

With the exception of Chapter 1, this book was derived directly from interviews. For the discussion in Chapter 1 of the evolutionary biology of sibling rivalry, see the following:

Douglas Mock and Geoffrey Parker, *The Evolution of Sibling Rivalry* (Oxford: Oxford University Press, 1998)
Douglas Mock, *More Than Kin and Less Than Kind: The Evolution of Family Conflict* (Cambridge, MA: Harvard University Press, 2004)
Martin Burd, Fredric Govedich, and Laura Bateson, "Sibling Competition in a Brood-Tending Leech," *Proceedings of the Royal Society of London, Series B (Biological Sciences)* 273 (2006): 2461–2466

The biblical exegesis was based on the translation of the Torah by Robert Alter, *The Five Books of Moses* (Norton: New York, 2004).

In Chapter 5, the information on family ownership of businesses comes from Robert Stewart, Andrea Kozak, Lynn Tingley, Jean Goddard, Elissa Blake, and Wendy Cassel, "Adult Sibling Relationships: A Comparison Across the Late Adolescent to Late Adulthood Years," *Personal Relationships* 8 (2001): 299–324.

The information on the prevalence of contentious adult sibling relationships comes from Robert Carroll, "Siblings and the Family Business," in *Siblings in Therapy: Life Span and Clinical Issues*, ed. Michael D. Kahn and Karen Gail Lewis (Norton: New York, 1988).

The information on the survival of family businesses comes from Ernest Doud and Lee Hauser, *Hats Off to You 2: Balancing Roles and Creating Success in Family Business* (Glendale, CA: Doud Hauser Vistar, 2004).

INDEX

Alcoholism, 83, 129, 218
   family businesses and, 107
   family separations and,
      206–207
   feeling responsible for, 63–64,
      67–68
Alienation
   introduced, 2
   taking time to undo, 155–156
   total or permanent, 201
   See also Separation
Ambition, driven by favoritism, 51
   See also Favoritism; Successful
      siblings
Anderson, Deborah and Ellen
   (siblings), 132–135, 199
Anger
   in abusive families, 139, 207
   and aggression, 54, 132,
      227–229
   contempt and, 2
   expressing to siblings, 97
   mutual, 171
   rage and, 130–132, 228–229
   resentment and, 51, 58, 112,
      152, 174–175
   ruling over oneself, 114–115
   siblings born with, 125–126
   violence and, 43, 130–132, 182,
      191, 192
Animosity, healing lifelong. *See*
      Healing process of siblings;
      Reconciliation process
Antipsychological, 242
Antisocial personalities, 187
Anxiety
   about place in parents'
      affections, 3
   from abuse, 95–96, 231–232

in asking for organ transplants,
   154
in avoidance of confrontation,
   65, 70–71
favoritism and, 51
initiation rites and, 37
money sponging siblings and, 80
removing barriers of, 249
Apologizing, in reconciliation
   process, 235–236, 241
Arboricide, 191, 192–193
Armor, chinks in, 202
Assisted suicides, 174–175, 221
Atkins, Larry and Bob (siblings),
   90, 94
Attention, parental
   ambivalence regarding, 148
   boys versus girls in, 145–146
   center of, 167, 172
   inadequate, 52
   mutual anger over, 171,
      241–242
   siblings vying for, 12, 105, 156
   when never challenging parent,
      118
   younger siblings getting, 203
Austen, Jane, 50

Babies of the family
   jealousy of, 111, 161–162,
      227–228, 238
   See also Favoritism
Bacteria, siblicide and, 11, 16
Beehives, siblicide and, 17
Ben (diner owner), 104
Benjamin (brother of Joseph), 31,
   37, 39, 40, 41
Bergman, Joan, 179–180
Betrayals